*choosing*
*Love or Anger*

# 4Days

*to a forever*

# Marriage

# Dr. Gary & Norma SMALLEY

choosing
*Love* or *Anger*

# 4 Days

*to a forever*

# Marriage

New Leaf Press

First printing: October 2011

New Leaf Press, P.O. Box 726, Green Forest, AR 72638

New Leaf Press is a division of the New Leaf Publishing Group, Inc.

ISBN: 978-0-89221-708-3

Library of Congress Number: 2011937093

Edited and Arranged by Craig Froman

Cover & Interior Design by Diana Bogardus
    Special thanks to Matt & Katie Gumm, Angela Jennings (Hill) & Jonathan Fiske Hill for their
    help with photographs. All other art from shutterstock.com.

Unless otherwise noted, Scripture quotations are from the New International Version of the Bible.

Please consider requesting that a copy of this volume be purchased by your local library system.

Printed in the United States of America

Please visit our website for other great titles:

www.newleafpress.net

For information regarding author interviews,
please contact the publicity department at (870) 438-5288

**New Leaf Press**
A Division of New Leaf Publishing Group
www.newleafpress.net

# What's in It for You?

A lot of people have advice for your marriage: talk show hosts, self-help gurus, family, friends, and even your pastor. It's easy to be distracted by the symptoms of marriage stress and "get fixed quick solutions" related to finances, infidelity, or parenting; but how often have you gotten out of one challenge only to be in another with the same issues as before?

This isn't about running from problem to problem trying to just stay ahead. *4 Days to a Forever Marriage* is about using a simple, easy choice that can transform your marriage into the lasting, loving connection you want it to be. Love or anger. It really does put power in your hands to determine the success of your relationship — no matter where you may be on the "marriage meter":

- "My marriage is good, and if it can be better, I want that!"
- "Things have changed, we've drifted apart, and I am not sure what is wrong."
- "It's so bad; we just fight all the time….I don't think we are going to make it."
- "I want what that couple has in their relationship."
- "I made a mistake — I chose poorly. My 'real' soulmate is out there. I just need to find 'the right one.'"

## Is it really that simple — love or anger?

Sure. The secret is in navigating the choices in a way that fosters real and meaningful communication. No time limit or special resources required — this is a solution for everyday marriage, dealing with the messy to the mundane, all with the goal of making sure you get the marriage you want and need.

# What Makes this Book Different

- ∞ Offers a non-situational approach that can work for any marriage. Seriously — any marriage! Master these two responses and it will help you survive life's crises with your relationship even stronger than before.

- ∞ Expertise from years of experience mentoring and counseling thousands of couples with all ranges of challenges — The Smalley's have seen and heard it all.

- ∞ Tips from an experienced couple who have survived multiple marriage seasons of their own: courtship, early challenges, raising children, health, ministry, and even financial pressures.

- ∞ An honest, open presentation from a ministry focused for decades on achieving marital success.

## Special Book Features:

- ∞ Practical steps for him and for her — with a great mix of helpful biblical wisdom.

- ∞ A two-person perspective from Gary and Norma — giving both sides of the issues from their own challenges and the insight that helped them resolve it.

- ∞ Directed introspection for you at the end of each chapter — and specialized guidance for every season of marriage.

- ∞ Tweet-style insights sprinkled throughout — quick and easy tidbits for your daily inspiration!

- ∞ Advice for: finding time to speak with your spouse, romantic ideas for $20 or less, Smalley fighting rules, the power of dreams, and much more!

# From People Like You:

When Gary Smalley taught us to treat each other as one who is highly valuable to God, our marriage began to heal. Today our marriage is a "safe" place because we began to practice honoring each other with words and in action.

*Jennifer — enjoying a vibrant second marriage of 13 years*

My marriage was in crisis then along came Gary. He took my wife and me out to lunch after church one Sunday and talked about changing the heart. We're still married and daily work on changing our hearts.

*Thomas — Married 30 years to my high school sweetheart*

Reading Gary Smalley's words profoundly impacted my view of my husband and my marriage. I love how he lets you know he's not perfect. Following his lead was easy and now the before and after picture of my marriage amazes me. To God be the glory!

*Louanne — after 14 years on our second marriage, we are in Big Love*

# From the Christian Community:

I've said it many times; joy is a choice! Well, Gary and Norma, my "forever" friends, have revealed clearly that love and anger are "choices" as well. So get the book now and choose to read it!

*Dr. Dennis Swanberg*
*America's Minister of Encouragement*

Gary Smalley has challenged and inspired me for years. His practical approach to living out the words of Jesus in a marriage is simple yet powerful. You will love his interactive approach to strengthen your marriage.

*Craig Groeschel*
*Founder and Senior Pastor of LifeChurch.tv*

Gary and Norma Smalley show you how to secure your marriage using Biblical principles they have practiced for their 40 plus years of marriage. In *4 Days to a Forever Marriage,* I found simple steps I will use to love and honor my wife more. It's a great gift for every engaged and married couple.

*Mark Batterson*
*Lead Pastor of National Community Church*

# Dedication:

We are so proud of each one of you in your desire to serve God and love people. May God continue to richly pour His grace into you and your family.

Roger & Kari Gibson

Michael

Hannah

Zoie Senait

Greg & Erin Smalley

Taylor

Maddie

Garrison

Annie

Michael & Amy Smalley

Cole

Reagan

David

—With love, Mom and Dad

Grandchildren are the crowning glory of the aged; parents are the pride of their children.

Psalm 17:5; NLT

*Gary & Norma with their grandchildren.*

I Corinthians 13:13

# Contents

> *Above all, love each other deeply, because love covers over a multitude of sins.*
>
> *1 Peter 4:8*

## Meet the Smalleys

We want to assure you, based on our own experience and that of thousands of other couples we've observed and talked to, that your marriage can get better and better as the years go by. We've now been married more than 40 years, and we're happier together today than we've ever been. But as happy as we are, we expect the future to be even brighter! You can have the same experience that we have shared with so many couples through our Smalley Relationship Center.

### Healthy or Hurting?

*4 Days to a Forever Marriage* was created to help you make the daily decision to choose love, which is focused concern for another, over anger, which in the context of marriage is focused concern for self and pride. By this we hope to help you strengthen your relationship every day from here on out. In fact, in your interactions with one another this choice of love or anger is the most discerning means to see the course of a marriage, whether it is healthy and thriving or perhaps becoming hurtful and destructive.

Make the right choices daily by taking this four-day challenge. Learn how to honor your spouse through the course of this precious time, beginning on day one with an understanding of the influence of loving words and actions. The following days bring to light aspects of loving communication and anger resolution, affection and intimacy, and discovering treasures in trials.

**Norma:** I'm a wife, the mother of three, and now a grandmother to ten grandchildren as well. (I also manage the day-to-day operations of our ministry, Smalley Relationship Center.) And for all the years of our marriage, our relationship has been a partnership. We've learned and grown together in every situation, good and bad. We've teamed up to begin transforming your marriage in just four days. We honestly and openly discuss our own challenges and solutions, and you can consider us your marriage coaches! Although the next chapter addresses men and women separately, reading both sections will not only help you understand yourself better, it will help you understand your spouse as well!

How could we do that effectively, we wondered — both of us writing but each from a different perspective? We decided that the best way was to invite you to "listen in" on our dialogue as we discuss topics on perceived needs, developing emotional word pictures, keys in communication, affection, romance, and more.

11

**Gary:** For as long as I've been trying to help families, honor has been the central theme of my message. It's the single most important key to healthy, successful relationships. Honor is a meaningful expression that represents the deepest respect and love.

Some time back, I—being a loving, sensitive husband whose whole ministry is based on the concept of honoring others—was talking to Norma on the phone, and in the course of our conversation I asked, "What do you need from me that I'm not giving you right now?"

She responded, "You don't know how to honor me." Naturally I laughed, assuming she was joking. I thought, *You can't be serious!* I said, "That's a good one! But what do you really need?" And she said, "No, I'm not kidding. You don't know how to honor me."

**Norma:** I realized that at that moment, Gary and I were thinking of love and honor in different ways. He was thinking globally—big picture—and from that perspective he does do a good job of caring for me. He really works at it, and I enjoy and appreciate it very much. But on this occasion, I was thinking of love in a far more specific way. I was focusing on some things Gary does that bother me that I would put under the heading of "manners." I want him to have good manners, which I consider to be an important part of how a husband honors his wife and others.

For example, like most women, I take a lot of pride in my home. The way it looks affects the way I feel and also reflects on me as a homemaker. So if Gary wants to show me love and honor, he should have the good manners to do his part to keep the house neat and picked up. Well, Gary has a home office that's right off our kitchen and is very visible from there. And he keeps—I promise this is no exaggeration—20 pairs of shoes on the floor in that office! Every time I look over there and see those, I feel as if I'm not keeping up the house the way I should. Just the other day, after working in the ministry office for 10 hours, I came home and found three pairs of his shoes sitting right in front of the TV in the family room!

**Gary:** Obviously, after all these years, we still need to work at this idea of loving each other. And it is work! In my mind, honor is a diamond. We started out with a rough, raw stone, and over the years we've made several major cuts and polishes, turning it into a beautiful gem. As far as I'm usually concerned, I'm doing a great job and it's ready to mount and display! Norma, on the other hand, because she knows me better than anyone, realizes that there are still some rough surfaces, and she sees them all every day.

**Norma:** That just goes to show what we said earlier, that no matter how long we've been married, we still need to work at our relationship and make the right choices. We never want to take each other or our marriage for granted. In fact, that might be one of the best lessons you could take away from this book.

# Before You Begin

As you work through the following chapters, we pray that the Lord will open your hearts to choose love over anger each and every day of your lives. Consider discussing the following questions with your spouse prior to beginning the first day. These will be revisited at the conclusion of the book:

1. What does a good relationship look like to you?

2. What hinders a good relationship?

3. Where is our relationship today on a scale of 1 to 10?

4. What would it take to make our relationship better?

Whichever way you decide to use the material, may you and your spouse turn your marriage into a lifelong expression of loving choices!

# 1

## Loving Words & Actions

DAY 1

**love**

*-noun, verb*

a deeply caring, profound sense of affection for another

# For the Husband

What is love? How do you honor your spouse? What does it look like in terms of living in a relationship? Loving your wife can mean many things to many people. It often means different things to a husband and wife at a given point in time.

> Love is patient, love is kind. It does not envy, it does not boast, it is not proud. It does not dishonor others, it is not self-seeking, it is not easily angered, it keeps no record of wrongs. Love does not delight in evil but rejoices with the truth. It always protects, always trusts, always hopes, always perseveres.
>
> —1 Corinthians 13:4-7

A husband may assume he knows what his wife wants, when she may actually want something entirely different. One of the best things a husband can do, then, is to ask his wife, "What does honor mean to you? How would you like for me to show you love?" When she tells him what she wants, he can act out of knowledge instead of mistaken assumptions and misplaced priorities.

As a husband growing an active marriage ministry and meeting commitments from work as an author, Gary Smalley learned a key lesson in love and honor when both his relationship with his wife and his ministry were challenged by what appeared to be great success.

**Gary:** One of the key ways a man can honor his wife is by thinking about how the commitments he makes will affect her before he makes them.

For example, I had come out with a new book, and the publisher asked me to go on a publicity tour to help generate some interest in it. Since I'm an outgoing person who loves to minister to people, I didn't have to be asked twice. This was an extended, intensive tour that kept me on the road for three long, hard months. But I was having a great time! A lot of good things were happening. Things were going so well, I was ready to sign up for a second tour.

Surely Norma would want me to do this, I figured. It's a good thing I didn't lock myself into that commitment before I talked it over with her.

**Norma:** Gary was having so much fun—and helping so many people on the tour—that he didn't realize what was happening at home. Emotionally, I was hurting. I felt as if I had fallen from second place in his priorities, after God, to about fifth. I don't get jealous of all the attention Gary gets in his work, but I am bothered when he pushes me out of my rightful place.

In addition, his being gone so much and speaking in so many cities was putting incredible strain on our ministry staff. They, like me, were frustrated with the prospect of a second tour.

**Gary:** When Norma first told me she was opposed to my going on a second tour, I actually thought she was trying to block my future success. Can you imagine? That's how blind I was to the impact the first tour was having. But after she explained things, and after the members of our staff helped me understand the burden they were carrying, I had no more desire to do the second tour. My fulfillment, after all, is in Christ, not in publicity tours.

**Norma:** Most of you husbands are asked all the time, like Gary, to make commitments that would have strong, direct impacts on your wives. Does that mean you should never make such a commitment? Of course not. Give her a chance to be your cheerleader or share her concerns. But the point is that you should think about the impact of the commitment on her—and better still ask her what she thinks of it—before you make it. That's showing love and honor to your wife.

*Ephesians 5:25*

## Strive for Love & Success

Like any challenge in your career or in sports, your marriage is subject to choices that determine its success or failure. When you make choices that show love and honor to your wife, you increase your chances for relationship success. And it helps if you learn to recognize what it looks like when your actions are not showing love or honor. By honoring these boundaries you can make the necessary adjustments so your marriage will stay on the right course. Men and women navigate relationships differently. What each of you needs from the other doesn't have to be a mystery. By simply determining what each of you needs from the other, you will be able to avoid a lot of conflict in the future. Remember, honor doesn't always mean some kind of action — it can also involve the words we choose to speak.

# The Strength and Power of Words

Women want to be connected to their husbands, but men are naturally more comfortable keeping their distance. For the relationship to thrive, husbands need to learn the skills of connecting by meaningful conversation and by listening to the feelings and needs of their wives.

Husbands should realize that the words they speak to their wives have awesome power to build up or tear down emotionally. Affirming words are like light switches. To speak a word of affirmation at the right moment is like lighting up a whole roomful of possibilities. A husband must learn to listen to the words of his wife, as well as the meaning behind the words. When a man learns to speak both the language of the head and the language of the heart, it can make tremendous positive changes in his own life and in the lives of his wife and children.

One simple way to honor your wife is by regularly showing that you appreciate her. Specific words of praise always score major points, but make sure they are sincere and don't go overboard. Flattery is insincere or excessive praise. It's rooted in motives of self-interest; it implies you want something from her. True praise, on the other hand, focuses more on character qualities and is not self-serving.

Men, when was the last time you looked your wife in the eyes and said, "I appreciate so much the things you do to make our house into a home and the time you give to the kids—you're terrific! I also appreciate your emphasis on relationships and all you do to build ours up"?

Not showing love and honor is what creates a distance in your relationship. Some husbands and wives have built a high wall between them over the years. Each brick is an unconfessed and unforgiven act that closed the partner's spirit a little more. Just as it took time to build the wall, it will also take time to tear it down. If a husband will take the initiative to go back and deal with as many offenses as he and his wife remember, they will find tremendous healing.

17

I want 2 b a genuine, loving, & tender husband who does not lecture. I'm choosing Love over Anger.

# Get Your Attitude in Action

When a woman sees her husband's willingness to accept correction rather than responding defensively in anger—a mark of someone who wants to gain wisdom—she's more willing to follow his leadership in the home because she values him more highly. If a man truly wants his wife to grow and the marriage to be strengthened, he should be the example of what he wants to see in her before saying anything to her.

An incredible amount of hard feelings and conflict could be avoided if husbands would resolve not to make any decision affecting their wives and the rest of their families without first getting their wives' input. When a wife is treated with tenderness and genuine love, she won't take advantage of the situation. The Scriptures teach that a husband is to cherish his wife, which basically means to protect her, especially in areas that cause her emotional or physical discomfort.

*Colossians 3:8*

When a man treats his wife carelessly, she's usually offended far deeper than he realizes. She begins to close him out, and if he continues to hurt her feelings, she will separate herself from him mentally, emotionally, and physically.

> Honor put into action regardless of the cost = genuine love.

A woman misses very little about her environment, which is probably the basis for that mysterious gift some have called intuition—and another reason a man should honor and value his wife. Because a woman's sense of value is so closely tied to the relationships around her, she's often gifted in helping her husband be more sensitive to what's really important beyond the immediate goal.

Honoring your wife means protecting her like an offensive lineman forming a wall of protection in front of his quarterback. In football, there are rules to protect the quarterback from injury. Honor is the biblical principle God designed to protect each mate from being unnecessarily injured.

Here's another secret to success. If you want to be considered great by your wife, start by learning to become a servant. Any time you promote her program or agenda over yours—without grumbling or complaining—you are sacrificially loving her.

**W**omen will remember not only when they were offended, but also what the offender was wearing when the offense occurred. By following these five steps after an offense, however—gentleness, understanding, confession, touching, and asking for forgiveness—a husband can begin to tear down the barriers that have sprung up to block the relationship.

Before marriage, differences attract BUT they may later repel. Value the differences as a gift that brings great balance.

## Assumptions vs. Understanding

The major stumbling block for most husbands in developing a lasting love for their mate is failing to meet her needs from her viewpoint. One can too easily assume the needs of a spouse based on one's own expectations and desires. Such perceived needs must be discussed and clarified over time in order to reach a true understanding of your mate.

Don't be surprised if your wife doesn't understand your efforts to improve at first. It took at least two years before Norma would admit I was really changing. Now she knows I'm committed to spending the rest of my life developing our relationship and meeting her needs.

**W**ives need consistent proof of change over a period of time in at least three areas before they will believe their husband's commitment: careful listening without justification or argument, quickness to admit error, and patience with her doubts.

A woman loves to build a lasting relationship with a man who cares about her enough to let her lean on him when she needs comfort. She needs a man who will understand her fears and limitations so that he can protect her.

Let your wife teach you how you can best meet her needs during a crisis or when she's discouraged and losing energy. Valuing his wife's differences, and even taking the time to be a student of her needs, does not diminish the husband's leadership or responsibility in the family.

# Built-in Fences

Your wife has "fences" that protect her privacy or need for emotional space. When you respect these boundaries, it shows that you honor her requests. And when you honor your wife, she will sense that nothing and no one in the world is more important to you. She won't have to wonder if she's number one—she'll know.

*When a wife expresses frustration, she will be more receptive to her husband's shoulders & arms than his mouth.*

A man needs to recognize the tremendous worth of his wife. Women have two incredibly important capacities because of the special way they're created. First, they have an intuitive desire to build meaningful relationships with those in their lives. Not only that, but they also have the capacity to recognize a healthy and intimate relationship. In a practical way, this means that a woman carries inside her a built-in marriage manual!

If a woman has had a poor relationship with her father, she may have a hard time relating to her husband. The husband needs to realize he didn't cause this problem or some of the other things with which his wife struggles. However, he is responsible for his wife, and it's his job to find out what she needs for health and well-being.

Jesus knew when His men were tired and needed to get away for some rest. One application for the husband is to be sensitive to when his wife needs a break from household responsibilities. He could offer to take care of the children for an evening so she can go shopping or do whatever else she desires.

Recognize your wife's uniqueness. Because men and women are created differently, we need each other in order to grow toward maturity and balance. A woman may have more intuitive relational skills, but one of the strengths of a man is that he can decide to draw on those skills by asking probing questions like these: What could we do in the next several days or weeks to bring our relationship closer to where we want it to be? How can I show love or honor to you today? How has anger impacted our relationship this week, and if so, how can we resolve the issue?

# For the Wife

Women tend to be better at honoring their mates than men do. Nonetheless, there are things wives can learn, too, that will help them to show honor to the most important person in their lives. One of the key ways a wife can honor her husband is to share in his interests—to get excited, at least to some extent, about the things that excite him.

**Norma:** One time years ago, Gary and I both listed what would be a dream vacation trip for us, then exchanged lists. So I've known all this time (more than a decade) what he would really like to do in this area—a sailing and fishing trip where he can catch his dinner and have it cooked right up fresh. Because it wasn't something that appealed to me, however, I didn't show any enthusiasm for it, and Gary didn't take that particular trip. Eventually, I saw that a trip like this was a way to honor Gary. He finally had his dream vacation with me at his side!

**Gary:** It meant a lot to me that Norma wanted to see that dream of mine come true and was willing to join me. She even organized it for me. I really do feel loved by that decision. Another way she honors me is that she has learned to validate the fact that I have an off-the-wall kind of personality, and she's learning not to criticize or try to change who I am. I seem to come up with a new idea for something several times a day. In the past, as soon as I threw out one of these ideas, she would start shooting it down, pointing out what was wrong with it and all the reasons why it couldn't possibly work. I felt as if my ideas were the clay pigeons at a skeet shoot, and she was the expert marksman! Now, however, she listens and lets me have the fun of stating my ideas without immediately jumping in and blowing them out of the sky.

**Norma:** For the first 25 years of our marriage, I didn't realize that Gary thinks out loud—talking about an idea is the way he processes things. I thought that rather than just brainstorming, he was fully intending to do whatever he talked about, and it was up to me to figure out how to make it happen. Once I finally understood his personality and the way he handles ideas, I also realized I didn't have to worry every time he came up with a new one. He wasn't really going to overturn our lives completely every couple of hours! Part of how I've been able to honor Gary, then, was in learning enough about him to understand (better, at least) how he thinks. And that, in turn, made it possible for me to honor him by hearing out his ideas completely before offering any comments. We're both a lot more fulfilled as a result.

## Your Starting Point

As a wife, you need to understand these differences between men and women:

By nature, a woman tends to relate to others on a more personal level, while a man tends to be more oriented to "challenge and conquer."

A woman finds much of her identity through her relationships, while a man usually finds his identity through his accomplishments.

A woman is usually much more in touch with her emotions, but a man is primarily concerned with the "facts."

The average woman speaks nearly 25,000 words a day, while the average man speaks only around 12,500!

Love = admitting you hurt his feelings & asking for his forgiveness.

## So, Draw Him a Picture...with Words

If you truly expect to have meaningful communication with your husband, you have to activate the right side of his brain so he can understand your feelings. One of the best ways to do this is with a word picture.

An emotional word picture is a communication tool that uses a story or object to activate simultaneously the emotions and the intellect of a person. In so doing, it causes the person to experience our words, not just hear them. A simple example of a word picture would be, "My week so far has made me feel like a puppy picked up by the scruff of its neck, because I feel carried along by circumstances beyond my control."

**W**hen your husband shares an idea with you that doesn't sit right, be careful how you respond. He needs the confidence and security of knowing you won't react in a severe or overly negative way.

Most men don't have all the "right brain" relational talents that most women do, but they can gain the knowledge and skills to become effective communicators. In fact, one of the strengths of men is that they can make a left-brain decision to develop those skills by asking probing questions (which is something they're good at).

Though your husband may not demonstrate or even realize it, he needs you to teach him about intimate relationships! Men can learn how to relate at a deep level, but only when they've chosen to communicate — a decision you can help your mate to make.

*23*

## Giving Thanks

Keep a mental list of little things your husband does that save you time and effort, and thank him for them as often as possible. When he feels he's meeting the "small" as well as the big needs of his family, his self-respect increases, and he will often begin to feel a deeper love for his appreciative wife.

Never belittle your husband's job or the importance of his activities at work. Nothing destroys a man's self-esteem more than to hear his wife cutting down his efforts to support her. And remember that being ignorant of what he does on the job may, in his eyes, be the same as belittling his work.

Every man has tremendous value. It's hidden at times, perhaps, but always there—a worth based on the incredible impact he has on every member of the family through his everyday actions and attitudes. Encourage him to remember how important he is and to make that impact positive and affirming.

# Choosing the Treasure

Treasuring is an attitude we carry in our hearts, a conviction we hold deep down inside. It's one big decision that plays itself out in 10,000 little decisions every day of our lives. This one giant choice to treasure your husband lights up a home like nothing else. Become a channel of God's love to your husband. Jesus calls on you to love God with your whole heart and your neighbor (especially your husband) as you do yourself.

*Matthew 22:37-40*

Every man needs to know that someone, somewhere in the world, cares about him. He needs to feel warm, friendly acceptance from a committed, intimate friend who will be devoted to him no matter what he does. In other words, just like you, your husband needs the security of genuine love. Be the person he knows is always in his corner.

As a wife, doing recreational things with your husband can be a key to keeping his interest. That doesn't mean you have to take up hunting or hang gliding, but picking an interest of his—and making it one you can share with him—can pay rich dividends.

Men need to feel appreciated. Many husbands think their biggest contribution to you and the family is the financial support they provide. One of the best ways to show your appreciation is to thank him for his faithfulness on the job. Even if you're providing part of the income (or most of it!), it's crucial that you show him how grateful you are for his provision.

> A wife skilled at meeting her husband's needs will become indispensable to him.

Let your husband know you're proud of him and you accept him even if you don't completely agree with the decisions he makes and the direction he's going. When your husband is down, don't react with disgust as though he has lost his masculinity. Maintain the attitude that he's important.

## Acceptance Turns Away Anger

Avoid being "hypersensitive" to every frown or smile from your husband. At all costs, put away anger if your husband doesn't follow through on developing the type of relationship you desire. Focus on what you have, not on what you don't have. No husband will make perfect decisions or be without fault. But using a variety of ways to express genuine appreciation or admiration for your mate can keep him from looking to someone else to meet that need.

Refrain from confronting your husband's deficiencies in anger. A man has a tendency to fight his conscience, and if you become his conscience, he'll either fight you or flee from you. Whichever route he takes, you've failed in your desire to spend more time with him.

Your husband might sometimes irritate you, belittle you, offend you, ignore you, or even nauseate you, but admiration looks beyond what he does to who he is. It's unconditional. Men gravitate toward those who admire them.

Your husband will usually gain more intimacy from what he "does" with you than from what the two of you talk about. So plan activities each week where you can bond by enjoying each other as you do something together.

25

Deciding someone is valuable is a major step in acting out our love for him or her. Love grows out of an attitude of honor.

# The Path to Less Stress…for Both of You

You and your marriage will experience less stress if you understand that men tend to be challenge-oriented and often lose interest once they've "conquered" or met the challenge. That's why they can be so romantic before marriage and afterward show little interest in romance. You can motivate your husband to love you by learning to be a courageous, persistent, and patient wife. As a completer and helper, you will need courage to help motivate change, gentle persistence to make sure it continues, and patience to wait on the Lord when change is long in coming.

Your husband needs to be made aware—in creative, loving ways—of how to meet your needs. Realize that your husband may well think he knows what you need. This perception can lead to frustration and discouragement for both of you. The more you clarify what you truly need, the more he will be able to love you. Remember, you're in the process of sharing with him how to love you, and he's in the process of learning. If you're on the same train, don't expect him to get to the destination before you do.

A woman's native ability in the area of relationships is her greatest resource. With it, she can lovingly and persistently help her husband fulfill life's most important responsibilities and reach the most crucial biblical milestones in life. Don't feel hurt and condemn your husband because he doesn't speak the "language of relationships" very well. To him, it's like a foreign language. Instead, help him learn to use it as fluently as you do.

By diminishing your expectations—by not expecting your husband to provide a level of fulfillment that only God can give—you free your husband of a burden you otherwise force him to bear, and you free yourself from unnecessary disappointment. This doesn't mean ignoring your needs or wants, just getting rid of your time limit and preconceived ideas about when and how those expectations will be met.

A man's competitive nature, when turned toward gaining a successful relationship, can cause dramatic growth in his marriage. Once the knowledge and skills of good relationships are in sight, he can go after them the same way he "conquers" a project at work.

Men need to know their advice is valuable. Welcome your husband's advice by . . .

- putting aside all other interests and giving him your full attention;

- focusing your eyes on him as he speaks;

- pointing out positive or helpful aspects of his advice;

- letting him have the floor until he has fully expressed his opinion;

- thanking him for the time he spent offering his advice.

## Choosing Love or Anger

We choose our actions and responses every hour of every day. Learn to distinguish and choose love by looking over the following traits of love and anger, and journaling or discussing how you will demonstrate love more than anger.

| *Love* | *Anger* |
|---|---|
| Patient | Anxious |
| Kind | Insensitive |
| Self-controlled | Impetuous |
| Forgiving | Vengeful |
| Merciful | Relentless |
| Compassionate | Selfish |
| Encouraging | Intimidating |
| Thankful | Ungrateful |
| Helpful | Spiteful |
| Cooperative | Obstinate |

27

# For the Husband

In your own words, summarize a principle from each portion of the day's insight. How will you apply these to your relationship?

The Strength and Power of Words _____

_____

_____

Get Your Attitude in Action_____

_____

_____

Assumptions vs. Understanding _____

_____

_____

Built-in Fences _____

_____

_____

What will you do today to show love to your wife & honor her needs? ___

_____

_____

_____

*Principle step for the day:* Promise to tell
your wife daily what you appreciate about her.
Promise yourself, not her, because she might develop
expectations and be hurt if you forget.

# For the Wife

In your own words, summarize a principle from each portion of the day's insights. How will you apply these to your relationship?

So, Draw Him a Picture with Words _____

_____

_____

Choosing the Treasure_____

_____

_____

Acceptance Turns Away Anger_____

_____

_____

The Path to Less Stress _____

_____

_____

What will you do today to show love to your husband & honor his needs?

29

_____

_____

_____

*Principle step for the day:* Many men will do
almost anything to gain the admiration of
others. They will literally
search for someone to love and respect them.
Make sure that someone is you.

# 2

## Communication and Resolving Anger

day 2

**com·mu·ni·ca·tion**

-noun

feelings or thoughts shared
through written, verbal, or
non-verbal language

## Communicating from the Word "Go"

*Gary:* A lot has been written and said about how to communicate in marriage. I should know—I've done my share of the talking in my previous books and seminars! But the fact is that it took me a long time to learn one of the most important communication skills—how to listen.

I especially needed to learn how to listen to Norma!

*My mouth will speak words of wisdom; the meditation of my heart will give you understanding.*

—Psalm 49:3

*Norma:* In the Bible, the Book of Genesis says God made the wife to be her husband's completer—to give him strengths and insights he didn't have on his own. As Gary's work has developed over the years, I've tried to be that completer for him, but he hasn't always listened because I've often had to say things he didn't want to hear! One of the areas where he didn't want to listen was the subject of how big and complex our ministry staff should (or shouldn't) become.

*Gary:* As the ministry began to really grow a number of years ago, with new opportunities opening up nearly every day, it seemed natural to me that our staff should expand to meet those demands. There were seminars to run, books to publish, film series to produce, small-group studies to develop, and so on. I was ready to build an empire! I started interviewing and hiring people to help turn my dreams into reality. Norma didn't think that was a good idea and told me so. I didn't agree and told her so. Before too long, however, events would prove she was right.

31

**Norma:** Gary is a wonderfully gifted man in so many ways. But one of those ways is not administration. Based on his natural strengths and weaknesses, I don't think God ever intended him to manage a large organization. There are other ministries and companies through which he can exercise his speaking and other gifts. Nonetheless, as he said, he wouldn't hear that from me and so he went about hiring people. Some of them lasted only six months before they left in frustration and disappointment. Finally, though Gary still wasn't convinced I was right, he could see there were problems, so he agreed to seek some outside counsel. A short time later, we went to dinner with Dr. James Dobson, whose own Focus on the Family ministry was already fairly large and continuing to grow.

**Gary:** We met him in a restaurant in Southern California. As soon as we were ready to get down to business, I told him, "Jim, I want a staff as big as yours," and I explained all the things I thought God was calling us to do. "Well," he said, "let me ask you a few things." Then he asked a series of questions meant to reveal what kind of administrator I would be—things like "Are you good with details?" and "Can you make hard decisions and communicate them to your staff?" As he posed those questions, I had to answer no to every one. And all the time we were talking, Norma was kicking me under the table and smiling at me.

**Norma:** From talking with a lot of women, I know Gary was far from alone at that point in being willing to accept an insight from someone outside the family that he had been rejecting from his wife. To his credit, Gary listened to Jim that day, and from that time forward we've kept our ministry staff small and done a lot of work through others, like book publishers and churches. That experience was also a part of his learning process—learning to listen to me, even when he wanted to disagree, with the belief that I might have some helpful insight that he didn't possess.

**Gary:** It took me a lot of years, but eventually I accepted the fact that I had better listen carefully when Norma speaks about my strengths and gifts, about people and projects, and so on. She knows me better than I know myself in some ways, and she has a wonderful intuitive sense about people and situations. As we look back on our time together now, we can see dozens and dozens of times when she has guided me, protected me, and kept me from doing foolish things. No less than a hundred times, I've thanked her for going through the pain of speaking up through the years when she knew I wasn't going to like what she needed to say. If you want your mate to be all the help to you that God intended, start today to really listen to—and take to heart—what he or she has to say.

## I Told You So

Words have awesome power to build us up or tear us down emotionally. Many people can clearly remember words of praise their parents spoke years ago. Others can remember negative, cutting words—in extraordinary detail. Communication within the family is like the body's circulatory system. When we stop listening to each other, it's as though the family suffers a stroke. We become disabled. Certain members no longer respond to other members.

It is such a lie to think you'll change your spouse. Expectations are the number-one reason people are not happy. We keep expecting things and people to make us happy.

Explain how you feel instead of demanding that your partner improve. Use "I feel" statements, but wait for the right time, and abandon the "you" statements and the "I told you so" statements.

In defeating the arguments and problems that can crop up around any home, try seasoning each day with a liberal sprinkling of praise: "You're so smart." "What a treasure you are!" "That's so creative!" "I'm praying for you." "You're wonderful!" "I'm with you all the way." "Thank you for all your help."

Set aside 15 minutes at the end of the day to catch up. See more ways to connect with your spouse on page 103.

Smalley Relationship Center

33

How quick we are to pick out the negative while ignoring five equally obvious positives! Unless we're careful, our body language and facial expressions will tend to minimize our praise while maximizing our criticisms. Make it your goal to praise your mate for something at least once each day.

Other approaches to criticism: Be soft—you can often say the hardest thing to someone, and he or she will receive it if you say it gently. Ask questions—help people discover for themselves what you're trying to say. Use those visual word pictures. Communication takes perseverance—and the very strength and courage of God's Spirit—to replace impatience, insensitivity, and self-preoccupation with loving communication patterns.

Plant seeds of praise/encouragement that can grow into mighty trees—pillars that uphold an entire life.

It's crucial that a husband listen to his wife's thoughts and feelings; even possible correction. Through listening to her, he can learn how to love her as Christ loves the Church, so that their relationship will blossom into the mature marriage God designed. We must let God change and transform us, and bring us happiness. We try to do it externally, but it won't happen that way.

Many things have to happen if you're going to agree on major decisions. Norma and I have had to reason together for long periods in order to discover the reasons behind each other's perspectives. A couple cannot survive if one person always makes decisions independent of the other. It takes longer to make a decision if you insist on discussion that produces unity, but it removes the danger of hasty decisions that can cause a couple future problems in their marriage.

Work to avoid judgmental attitudes like "How stupid!" "Oh no, that would never work!" or "You'll never understand!" If you criticize your mate in a condescending manner, you're actually pushing him or her further away from you. No one enjoys being with a disrespectful person. And no one likes to be criticized. However, if you sandwich your criticism between two slices of sincere praise, you'll be amazed at the difference in your mate's reactions.

Proverbs 15:28

# How to Bridge the Differences

As mentioned earlier, an emotional word picture is a communication tool that uses a story or object to activate simultaneously the *emotions* and the *intellect* of a person. In so doing, it causes the person to *experience* our words, not just hear them. You might think of them as vivid metaphors or similes. They can be as simple as stating, "I feel like I'm in a jungle surrounded by tigers," if expressing fear or anxiety at work.

How do you honestly tell the one you love about something you find displeasing or aggravating without prompting that familiar defensive stare or indifferent shrug? You can help your mate become more sensitive to the problem by using a word picture rather than direct confrontation. Use examples that interest him or her, such as hobbies, everyday objects, or imaginary stories.

A lot of men avoid soft words and tender comfort because they've never been taught how to use them. Nor do they understand the positive effects those things will have on their wives and the sense of well-being they themselves will receive.

People who consistently use word pictures to point out the faults of others are mis-using this communication method. They may make you feel terrible with their words and somehow convince you it's your fault. Word pictures are to be used to convey how you feel, not to attack the other person.

The communication bridge between you and your spouse can be an emotional word picture, which can be a tremendous help in adding depth and impact to your conversations. Added to this, consistent, gentle touching is a powerful way

Emotional word pictures help whittle many problems down to size. Paint vivid pictures with your words.

to increase feelings of security, prime the pump for meaningful communication, and set the stage for emotionally bonding and romantic times. That's because a gentle hug is a powerful *nonverbal word picture* of love.

Meaningful communication is sharing your feelings, goals, and ideas—your very personhood. But it isn't always easy to express those deeper things to one another. That's where the right word picture can help to bring your thoughts to life, activating your mate's emotions as well as intellect.

## The Art of Timing

There's more to effective communication than putting together and then practicing the right message. Picking the right *time* and *place* to convey it is also crucial. In a marriage, meaningful words bring life-giving water to the soil of a person's life. In fact, all loving relationships need the continual intake of the water of communication or they simply dry up. No marriage can survive without it.

> Healthy communication is the lifeblood of love. "Lord, show us where we can listen more and the words that will honor each other."

If a man is to be truly effective in his relationships both at home and at work, he needs to develop the ability to speak the "language of the heart" (facts *and* feelings). Right there under the same roof is a woman who can help him learn that skill, if he is willing to listen to her.

Without meaning to, we can communicate nonverbally that other people or activities are more important to us than family. You've heard of football widows. How about golf orphans? Those who know us best provide the best correction. In particular, our mates, who were designed by God to complete us, are most sensitive to the areas in which we need help.

We also need to give praise and thanks to each other for special acts of kindness. Many people complain that their mate is strangely silent when they do something above and beyond the norm.

The Salt Principle is a method of gaining and holding a person's attention by arousing curiosity. It's a way to create a thirst for constructive conversation in which both you and your spouse can learn about each other's needs. First, identify the need or concern to be discussed, and then identify areas of high interest to the other person—areas you can tap into to pique interest.

One of the easiest ways to reduce misunderstandings and commu-nication friction is to share only a few thoughts with someone and then allow the person to repeat back what he or she thinks you said, much as would happen when you place an order at a fast food drive-through. This method will also improve your listening skills.

Added benefits to this kind of drive-through talking: (a) It gives you a chance to fully understand what the other person is saying before you respond, which also prevents tuning out the other person while he or she is talking; (b) it validates the other person and his or her opinions. When you not only listen but also repeat back what someone says, you communi-cate that the person and his or her opinions are important to you and worth taking seriously.

What are the five levels of communication?

1. *Clichés:* "How's it going?" or "What's up?"
2. *Facts:* "Looks like rain today" or "Sure is hot out."
3. *Opinions:* "I think the Raiders are going to win the Super Bowl" or "Your mother is interfering."
4. *Feelings:* "How do you feel about this?" or "I love you."
5. *Needs:* "What do you need to be happy?" or "I really need a hug from you."

The key to close-knit communication is to make conversa-tions "safe," where opinions, feelings, and needs can be treasured and valued.

# Those Days Are Gonna Come

**Gary:** Conflict is inevitable in any close relationship, including marriage. When you put together two people, male and female, from different backgrounds, with different customs and traditions, with varying expectations and dreams—disagreements are *going* to happen. The key issue is how you're going to deal with them.

**Norma:** We've found that sometimes conflicts come to a head quickly, and sometimes they build up over a long period. In our case, one issue developed over 30 years before it was resolved. The problem was that Gary started snoring, and it got worse as time went on. At first it was only irritating, even a little amusing. But as Gary's volume increased, my patience decreased! After a while, I realized he might actually have a serious medical problem known as sleep apnea. He would literally stop breathing for a few seconds as he slept, then begin again with a start, waking up a little in the process. As a result, neither one of us was getting much quality sleep.

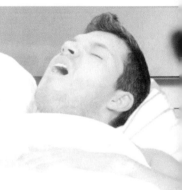

**Gary:** Like a typical man, however, I didn't think the problem was all that serious. And I certainly was in no hurry to go to a doctor! I had to acknowledge, however, that neither of us was sleeping very well. But what finally drove me to seek medical help was when Norma said she would need to move into a separate bedroom if I didn't get help! She had reached the point where she thought that was the only way she could get a little rest at night. I went to a sleep clinic, where they determined that I do, indeed, have sleep apnea. And they prescribed a breathing machine that forces air into my mouth and lungs while I sleep. It was incredible! The difference between "before" and "after" was like the difference between night and day. I soon found I had far more energy, a better ability to concentrate, and much less irritability than before.

*James 1: 19*

**Norma:** Our experience with Gary's sleep apnea has taught us a couple of things about marital conflict. First, if there's frequently or sometimes even constantly a level of friction or tension between you and your spouse, it may have a *physical* cause. So before you draw negative conclusions about each other's character or cooperativeness, look into that possibility. Solving your conflict could take a whole different direction from what you now think is needed if there is, in fact, a physical problem. (Conditions like sleep apnea, hormonal imbalances, and high blood pressure are more widespread than most people realize.) Second, when there is a conflict, we have to focus on the *problem* and look for solutions to it rather than focusing on the other person. Before Gary finally went and got treatment for his sleep apnea, I'll admit there were times when I got upset with him for not taking appropriate action and so forcing me to live with his continued snoring. But most of the time, I was able to keep things in a more healthy perspective. His apnea was the problem, not Gary himself. If I had let myself get mad at Gary about it too often, we might have ended up sleeping in different *houses*.

**Gary:** That brings up another point that can't be made too often: If a husband and wife are going to keep happily together for a lifetime, they simply *must* learn to give, ask for, and receive forgiveness. We *will* hurt each other from time to time, sometimes on purpose and sometimes without knowing it. If those injuries aren't forgiven, the spirit of the person who was hurt will close, making real intimacy next to impossible. Because of living with me, Norma has had to become an expert at offering forgiveness!

**Norma:** Gary knows I've needed to be forgiven my share of the time, too. But I absolutely agree that a willingness to forgive and to seek forgiveness when needed is one of the most crucial foundation stones in any marriage.

## Unresolved Anger

How destructive bottled-up resentment can be! Anger has many
tragic consequences in a marriage. It creates distance and pushes
us into darkness. It can tie our emotions and decisions into knots.
We may not be able to keep anger from cropping up as an instanta-
neous and instinctive reaction to some pain or problem, but we can
make a decision to keep it from staying in our lives and poisoning
our attitudes or the attitudes of our loved ones.

Philippians 1:27

Constant disagreement can only weaken a marriage
relationship. That's probably why Paul emphasized
having oneness of spirit and mind in the Church.
He likened the struggle for oneness to a team of
athletes striving to reach the goal.

In relating to others, are you shifted to
one extreme or the other? Are you camped in
the far reaches of the confrontative life, easily
issuing commands and criticism but not given
to caring actions? Or do you rarely move beyond an unhealthy avoidance lifestyle, unwill-
ing to confront someone to take the lead?

Unresolved anger in your
home is more toxic than
the radon gas! Commit to
resolving anger to secure
a forever marriage.

The build-up of unresolved anger results in
a closed spirit. Selfish anger is the negative
emotion we feel when a person or situation
has failed to meet our needs, blocked our goals, or fallen short of
our expectations. If you are constantly dishonoring your spouse for
one reason or another, it will usually close his or her spirit.

Anger creates distance, and distance destroys relationships. It
causes husbands and wives and parents and children to drift away
from each other. Home becomes little more than a dormitory with
hostile roommates. No matter how hard we work at the relational
"glue" that bonds our families together, anger is like fingernail pol-
ish remover that instantly dissolves that bonding.

# What Creates Conflict?

There's no way to overcome our weaknesses without knowing our strengths. Why? Almost without exception, our weaknesses are a reflection of our strengths being pushed to an extreme.

Many family conflicts are caused by viewing another person's strengths as weaknesses. A clear view of what naturally motivates another person can open the door to greater compassion, patience, compromise, and caring.

We may think people make us angry, but most of the time they simply reveal our own selfishness. What usually makes us angry is our lack of control over people and circumstances. Anger is inevitable in a marriage. Couples who gain skills at "keeping their spirits open" to each other and at dealing with anger in a constructive way take giant strides toward intimacy.

The "issue" is the first level of conflict. If two disputing parties can keep talking on the issue level, discussing the merits of each position and thinking through possible compromises, the tension could actually be constructive rather than destructive. Because a woman's need for a close, meaningful relationship is often greater than a man's, she is more sensitive to words and actions that can weaken a relationship.

There are five main reasons for conflict in the average relationship.

*Power and control:* When both parties are fighting for control or resenting not being able to take control, there's conflict.

*Individuality:* When one person tries to change or manipulate his or her partner, and the other resists, there's conflict.

*Distance:* When one person begins pulling away or putting up walls and defenses, he or she begins to distrust, and the need for self-preservation arises.

*Distrust:* When one or both people feel unsafe expressing their feelings or needs, there's conflict.

*Unmet needs:* When one partner feels his or her needs are not being met, again there's conflict.

41

*You can't fight in ANGER. You must learn to fight in LOVE of your spouse.*

# Discovering the Hope of Resolution

When you boil down a lot of destructive arguments, what you often find is a simple lack of facts. The conflicts begin when an individual sees something that bothers him and then draws a conclusion. But what he *thinks* he sees may not be true at all. There's nothing new about this advice. James, the Lord's brother, wrote, "My dear brothers and sisters, take note of this: Everyone should be quick to listen, slow to speak and slow to become angry."

Clearly understanding our God-given temperaments brings to light common causes of family disharmony, provides handles for resolving long-standing friction in the home, dramatically increases our feelings of value for our loved ones and friends, and gives additional reasons to honor God. Usually, by being soft, genuinely seeking to understand what happened, admitting when we're wrong, and specifically asking for forgiveness, we can see anger begin to drain away quickly in another.

The most insecure people are those who can't distance themselves from their loved ones enough to discipline them. Loving discipline may put a temporary emotional distance between people, but if we balance that hard-side correction with softness, we won't lose love. If anything, we'll enrich it.

Survey after survey shows that the number-one reason for mate selection is the *differences between* individuals. But differences can become a devastating source of conflict in a marriage. Learning to recognize and value each other's perspectives is one of the most positive things we can do.

When we have offended someone, we must give that person a chance to respond. *True restoration is confession of wrong* plus *forgiveness granted.* Even when crises come from external sources, we must be careful not to close the spirits of those around us. When we are under stress, we can react harshly to our mate and close his or her spirit. As we attempt to open our spouse's spirit, our body language, muscles, facial expressions, and tone of voice must become soft, gentle, and caring. By doing this, we're saying that he or she is valuable, that we know something is wrong, and that we are open to listen.

To reopen a person's spirit requires learning to listen beyond the words to the hurt feelings behind them.

Like few other emotions, anger restricts and binds us, tying us in eternal knots. Forgiveness, on the other hand, sets us free from those bonds, untying the knots that hold us captive. The Lord Jesus said, "Forgive, and you will be forgiven."

A couple in crisis should seek out correction through counseling. It is difficult at first, and humbling. Yet what is that small discomfort and embarrassment compared to the years of love, companionship, and happy memories they will share for the rest of their lives? *Only the wise seek correction.*

Keeping our "heads together" in stressful times is something like a foxhole experience. Those who have endured the horrors of trench warfare often remain friends for life, even though their ordeal may have lasted only a few weeks or months. Why? Because shared experience, whether pleasant or unpleasant, creates the common ground in which deep-rooted relationships germinate and grow. The greater the intensity of the experience, the greater the potential for bonds of love and intimacy that can bind us to one another in a beautiful relationship called a close-knit family.

Do not be threatened by the presence of conflict, but use it as a flashing road sign that gets your attention to do whatever is necessary to resolve it at some point.

43

Family crisis can't be scheduled, but you can—you must —make sure family activities get high priority on your yearly schedule.

## To Open a Closed Heart

There are five keys or attitudes that open a closed heart:

1. Become gentle; demonstrate tenderheartedness.
2. Understand what the other person has gone through, listening carefully not only to what is said, but also to how it is said. What has caused the anger?
3. Acknowledge that the person is hurting, and admit when you have been offensive.
4. Touch the other person gently.
5. Ask for forgiveness.

Are you still hesitating to knock down old walls of anger and put in a doorway of tenderness to your home—a door that opens to energizing words, gentle touching, and courageous forgiving?

## Choosing Love or Anger

We choose our actions and responses every hour of every day. Look over the following attributes of love and anger so you can choose wisely:

| *Love* | *Anger* |
| --- | --- |
| Stays calm when dealing with issues. | Speech becomes hasty when agitated. |
| There is a feeling of relaxation and peace. | Muscle tension causes head, stomach, and back discomfort |
| The conversation is focused on the issue. | Sarcasm is used to avoid the issue. |
| There is a desire to resolve the concerns. | There is a desire to win or retaliate if a win is not possible. |
| Silence is used to listen intently. | Silence is used as a form of punishment. |
| Physical touch is employed to comfort and relax. | Physical touch is used to harm or threaten the other. |
| The name of the spouse is held in highest regard. | The name of the spouse is used in a degrading way. |
| Finding resolution is of utmost importance in a crisis. | Placing blame is of utmost importance in a crisis. |

Whoever would foster love covers over an offense, but whoever repeats the matter separates close friends.

~ Proverbs 17:9

In your anger do not sin. Do not let the sun go down while you are still angry.

~ Ephesians 4.26

45

# For the Husband

In your own words, summarize several principles from each portion of the day's insights. In what way can you live these out?

Communicating from the Word "Go" _____

_____

_____

_____

_____

Those Days Are Gonna Come _____

_____

_____

_____

_____

Take a few moments and talk about your responses with your wife \_\_\_\_\_

_____

_____

_____

_____

*Principle step for the day:* Communicate humility. At times, some people act as if they know all the answers. It's important that a man be willing to learn and grow.

# For the Wife

In your own words, summarize several principles from each portion of the day's insights, and note how you will apply these to your relationship.

Communicating from the Word "Go" _____

_____

_____

_____

_____

Those Days Are Gonna Come _____

_____

_____

_____

_____

Take a few moments and talk about your responses with your husband __

_____

_____

_____

_____

47

*Principle step for the day:* Be gentle.
Gentleness (a willingness to decrease our lectures and increase
our tender expressions of love)
is a key to marital growth. Tenderness acts like a
firebreak to an advancing, angry fire.

# 3

## Affection and Intimacy

## Day 3

**in·ti·ma·cy**

*-noun*

a closeness developed with
another through continual loving
interactions that include physical
or verbal signs

# Intimacy: The Real Thing

**Gary:** When we say the word *intimacy*, most people immediately think of sex. But the physical act of coming together in marriage is only one aspect of intimacy. And in some ways, it's not even the most important aspect. (I know, you may find it hard to believe that a guy is saying that seriously, but hear me out.) The real definition of intimacy between two people is that they feel safe enough with each other to share their feelings and needs. If a husband and wife have that kind of intimacy, they won't have much trouble with sexual intimacy (unless, of course, there's a physical problem).

> "Haven't you read," he replied, "that at the beginning the Creator 'made them male and female' and said, 'For this reason a man will leave his father and mother and be united to his wife, and the two will become one flesh'? So they are no longer two, but one flesh. Therefore what God has joined together, let no one separate."
>
> —Matthew 19:4-6

**Norma:** Going by that definition of intimacy, I have to say that we really didn't have it for the first 20 years of our marriage. It took me that long to realize the importance of sharing my feelings and to feel safe enough to do it. For example, when we got married, I moved to Gary's town and started attending his big church. We were surrounded by "his people." I wanted them to see clearly that he really cared for me. But he never showed me any affection in public.

It was frustrating and disappointing, yet I didn't say anything. Partly because I thought, *That's just the way he is,* and partly I thought he should just know I was hurting—it seemed so obvious to me.

49

**Gary:** There's a good lesson for us men in that, since we're the ones who most often are cool toward our mates in public. Namely, we can simply ask our wives, "What would you like me to do to show publicly that I love you?" And wives, if your husband *doesn't* ask that question or just isn't doing what you'd like (even if it's only holding hands as you walk together), please take the initiative to *tell* him—in a loving and gentle way, of course. Please don't expect him to read your mind!

**Norma:** I'm reminded of another thing we've learned that can greatly increase marital intimacy. In our case, I would say it has doubled it! I used to get real excited when Gary would be asked to speak on a cruise, at a beach resort, or at some other nice vacation-type spot, and I was invited to go along. My thought would be that when he wasn't speaking, this would be a romantic, intimate getaway for the two of us. But I never told Gary that was my expectation. Again, I thought he should just know. Then, what happened *every* time was that about two days into the trip, Gary would want to start talking about setting goals and solving problems. I would be crushed, my dream shattered. Then I would withdraw from him physically and emotionally, because I knew that kind of discussion would be long and intense.

**Gary:** We'll talk in the next few pages about a couple of the things that have helped to develop more of a sense of security in our relationship. But one thing we've learned about how to increase intimacy in a situation like those trips is to simply agree beforehand on what we will and won't discuss. Couples often use a date night to catch up on issues and concerns between them. That's almost certain to *escalate* arguments rather than resolve them. Fortunately, I finally figured that out.

**Norma:** A woman equates "date" with "intimacy," which is why she looks forward to it so much. But when the conversation turns to dealing with issues instead, it kills that feeling and ruins the evening as far as she's concerned. What a simple thing it is to have an agreement before a date or a special vacation about what you will and won't talk about! Yet I can say without hesitation that it has increased our intimacy and our enjoyment of those times together, by at least 100 percent. Give it a try in your marriage.

# What's on Your Menu?

Communication is the single most effective way to deepen intimacy in any relationship, whether it's with your mate, family, friends, or on the job. Just as food is essential to a healthy body, intimate communication is essential to a healthy relationship. Generally, our communication is based on what we consider to be within our safety zone. It's incredibly safe to exist on clichés or by simply stating facts. Most conflicts begin to enter into the picture when we share opinions, feelings, or needs.

When you go to a restaurant, you request items off a menu. The same principle can be applied to a relationship. Request what you want from your mate—for example, a daily hug, help around the house, or appreciation for a job well done. Decide what's most important in your marriage, and put those things in writing. One menu item I suggest you include is an agreement that during an argument, you'll both list all the positive and negative aspects of the issue at hand. Seeing both sides can bring about a quicker resolution and also the unity you both desire.

MENU

1. Daily Hug

2. Help around the House

3. Thank You's

4. Encouraging Word

5. Kiss Goodnight

During an argument, list all the positive aspects of the issue at hand.

1 John 3:18

It's crucial that we develop healthy relationships. Doctors have found that tension from a poor marriage or friendship can actually cause illness and shorten a person's life! Not only that, but our children also gain or suffer from the model we provide them every day. One of the keys in any healthy relationship is a willingness to say, "I'm more interested in understanding what you're saying than in thinking of what I'm going to say once you're done talking."

A husband and wife need to establish a routine pattern of meaningful communication—times of sharing feelings, hopes, dreams, and fears. "Weather report" comments like "How's it going?" "How was the traffic today?" and other safe questions aren't enough. Every day, spouses need to add the water of well-spoken words to keep their relationship strong and healthy.

In a nurturing and healthy relationship, you perceive that your ideas and insights are valuable, and you learn how to negotiate and listen to the other person's views. You hear things like "What did you say?" "You always know the right thing to say," or "Let's talk about this."

In a healthy relationship, not only are you encouraged to feel, but you're also sensitive to others' feelings. You perceive that how you feel is valuable and that you're safe when sharing your feelings. You might hear things like "How do you feel about this?" "It's okay to feel like that," or "What can I do to make you feel better?"

When you honor your spouse above yourself, you develop close-knit feelings of belonging. In this atmosphere, you spend a great deal of quality time together. You might hear things like "Let's spend some time together," "What can I do to become closer to you?" or "What can I do to make you feel closer to me?"

When you and your spouse agree to live in oneness, you're consequently willing to spend more time listening and discussing in order to resolve important issues and so build intimacy. Whenever a husband and wife agree on the main areas of their lives, they become bonded together and achieve a unique strength. *Two people united are much stronger than one.*

> Frequent praise builds intimacy. The simplest way to make your spouse feel good is to say, "Well done!"

One way to cherish our mates is to help them become fulfilled as people. We can do this by discovering their personal goals and looking for ways to help them reach those objectives. We all love knowing someone is pulling for us. We should discuss our roles in marriage and what areas we need encouragement with. We should choose areas based on genuine love and not on expectations that have never been discussed.

## It Doesn't Begin in the Bedroom

A marriage can't be sustained with romance alone. But added to security, meaningful communication, and meaningful touch, it can be a tremendous source of energy and growth.

Wise husbands and wives will take time to practice small acts of touching: holding hands in a walk through the mall, stopping to rub your mate's shoulders for a moment, taking the time to gently hold your spouse at the door on your way out. These small but important acts can work like "super bloom" to a plant and green out a relationship.

The most successful relationships are those in which each person feels safe sharing his or her *feelings* and *needs*. This is where our personalities and parenting histories strongly affect us, because many of us are fearful or uncomfortable about sharing such intimacies. Life is more predictable—more secure and stable—when you know that both of you are working toward a loving, lasting relationship. This is the foundation for true intimacy.

Many men don't realize it, but more than 80 percent of a woman's need for meaningful touch is nonsexual. Sex does not begin in the bedroom. It actually starts in the everyday acts of truthfulness, consistency, kindness, touching, and talking that build a growing desire in a woman.

No one can long ignore considerate, loving actions. Make your mate feel special and you increase his or her desire to do the same for you.

Genuine love doesn't necessarily spring from feelings. Its basis is primarily a concern for the welfare of another. Although the feelings of affection will follow, genuine love is initially an action directed toward fulfilling another person's needs. Persistent love—like the dripping of water on a rock—can wear away a person's resistance. It's nearly impossible to stay angry with or emotionally distant from someone who unconditionally loves and values you.

*Song of Solomon 8:6*

So many men and women treat each other as objects to be used. They may not verbalize it, but they maintain an inward conviction that their mate should do things that have never been discussed. This is like steadily pouring acid on intimacy. From time to time, my wife and I get together on a date, for breakfast out or just a retreat from home. During that time, we list our personal goals and commit ourselves to helping each other fulfill those desires. I feel so satisfied knowing that my wife is committed enough to sacrifice for my goals and that I have the same commitment toward her.

One way intimacy is blocked is when lives are filled with unhealthy behavior—poor health choices or sexual addictions that affect our daily conduct. To change those habits and addictions, we should first recognize our mistakes and admit when we're at fault. Second, we must keep an attitude of wanting to improve. Third, we should share our feelings and needs with our mate and seek his or her understanding and support.

Keeping your written relationship menu posted in a prominent household location provides a continual reminder of which values and rules you're working toward. It generally takes about 30 days to start a new habit. So if you're regularly working on attaining your goals, it will only take a month before you notice significant changes in your relationship.

> True happiness comes by reaching out to others with a desire for them to feel love from us.

## 4 ways of building intimacy

1. Stop waiting for things to get better —make a decision to work on them.

2. Acquire and practice new attitudes and skills that lead to fulfilling relationships.

3. Commit to changing your own behaviors first, without expecting your partner to change his or hers.

4. Support each other in your efforts so that neither of you feels alone or inferior.

Song of Solomon 8:7

## Keep the Flame Burning

**Gary:** In this day and age, security in the marriage relationship almost seems to have gone the way of the public pay phone. Roughly half of all marriages end in divorce, and the statistics are about the same among Christians as they are in society at large. Yet feeling secure in the relationship is vital to true romance. How can you give yourself fully and without reservation to your spouse unless you're confident he or she will still be with you, loving and supporting you, next week, next year, ten years from now, and so on until the day that death finally separates you?

**Norma:** One way I've tried to build security in our marriage is that I've consciously and deliberately never used the words *hate* or *divorce* or *leave* with Gary, even in our most heated "discussions." I'll admit I *thought* the words on a number of occasions in years gone by. But I've seen the devastation done to individuals—men and women as well as children—and families by separation and divorce, and I never want any part of that. Even more, when I vowed on our wedding day to love and remain faithful to Gary, I was making that promise to God. I was making it to Gary as well, but I was especially making it to God, and I take that very seriously.

55

**Gary:** Another thing that has helped to build security in our relationship is that *we pray together* about anything in our family or ministry that looks challenging. There's a great sense of peace and oneness that comes from going to God together and placing a difficult matter in His hands.

We also know that when we're both seeking His will for a particular concern, we're on the right track to finding a good answer, because self-centeredness and ego have been taken out of play. We both want what's best for each other, for our marriage, for our family, or whatever the case may be.

**Norma:** It's nice to get flowers and to go out for fancy dinners. Those kinds of things do develop the feelings of romance that are so enjoyable, and I certainly like it when they're a part of our relationship. I've learned, however, that as nice as the feelings of romance are, they're no substitute for the security of a rock-solid commitment. Knowing that your love and your marriage will truly last "till death do us part" is the greatest feeling of all! During hard times, when I don't *feel* love toward Gary, I always remember that feelings change so many times during the day because situations change—but my decision to love him was a commitment for life.

**Gary:** Intimacy does not start in the bedroom; it has its fulfillment in the bedroom. Romantic expressions shared throughout your days can keep the sense of warmth and desire alive even when difficult times arise. The small things, good or bad, often are the ones that shape your relationship in the long term.

## Is Your Home Secure?

Ephesians 5:21–33

A marriage needs security to grow and thrive. To use a different analogy, the first structural support that holds up a meaningful relationship is found in that one word—*security*. Security is the assurance that someone is committed to loving and valuing us for a lifetime. It's a constant awareness that whatever difficulties we face, we'll work to overcome them together.

Security means we're fully committed to the truth and make a decision daily to be open to correction. We build security into our relationship each time we speak the truth, go out of our way to encourage our spouse, listen without lecturing, or give him or her a gentle hug.

A gardener—nurturer—has a responsibility not only to find out what's wrong with a plant, but also to do whatever is necessary to nurse it back to health. In Ephesians 5:21–33, we see this picture as a role of the husband. A character of honesty and serving must be deep-rooted to survive; it reaches way down into the soil of consistent living. It isn't a short-term change of behavior that makes an impression on your mate; *it's a life.*

Every enduring marriage involves an unconditional commitment to an imperfect person —your spouse.

A key to blending friendship with romance is to take the time to explore each other's interests and then share in them. Conversely, all it takes to see the romantic spark doused with buckets of cold water is to expose major impurities in one's character.

When you speak of a man's personal power, you immediately think of words reflecting character like *warmth, sensitivity, dependability, determination, genuine compassion,* and *caring.* A man will do almost anything to gain the admiration of others. The most important person from whom he wants it is his wife. Some women think that because their husbands are admired by others in their professions, they don't need it from their wives. That's a serious mistake.

Take the initiative occasionally to suggest a specific time to talk together. For example, set up a breakfast or dinner out with just the two of you. Let your convictions show. Meaningful conversation is crucial in developing a growing and loving relationship.

Design togetherness times that incorporate your spouse's interests. These may involve athletic events, musical concerts, museum trips, meals out, fine arts and entertainment, vacations, and so on.

Once a man can see the advantages in making a choice (the facts), he can often commit himself regardless of his feelings. For instance, even on a day when he doesn't necessarily "feel" like doing something (like spending a half hour in meaningful conversation with his wife), he can still make a decision to do so.

> Raise the passion level in your marriage by increasing the purity of your character.

The key to a close-knit marriage is maximizing the times together and minimizing the times apart. Our culture has a tendency to emphasize "doing your own thing" rather than marital closeness. The more activities you can do as a couple, the better are the chances that you'll develop a deep, lasting relationship. Can you imagine the ecstatic feeling you would have if your mate volunteered the question, "How can I become a better mate?" The honor you would feel would be overwhelming. So how about asking the question yourself?

How can we turn our negative thoughts to positive ones before they affect our sense of worth and become a hurtful part of our self-image? By developing a grateful attitude. One of the most attractive qualities a person can have is a spirit of gratefulness. In marriage, providing a deep sense of security for your partner is like bathing him or her in warm sunlight. That means convincing your mate in a variety of ways that, no matter what, you'll always be there to care for him or her.

Wives tell me they admire and honor a husband who admits he's wrong, especially when he openly seeks his wife's advice on how to improve. Many a husband has refused to listen to his wife's correction because of hang-ups over her choice of words.

> Creative and consistent praise nurtures a love-filled marriage.

What increases security in a marriage?

- Saying "I love you" regularly
- Making long-range plans together
- Cultivating a pattern of thoughtfulness
- Valuing each other's thoughts and feelings
- Demonstrating a strong commitment to Christ and to the spiritual health of your family

Romance is the process of keeping your courtship/dating alive long after the wedding day.

## Making Touch Meaningful

Couples need to create emotional bonding times. Keeping the flames of romance alive may not always seem as important as security or meaningful communication, but it is. Consistent positive times of emotional bonding can add tremendous stability to a home. Remaining tender during a trial is one of the most powerful ways to build an intimate relationship.

*Song of Solomon 4:11*

Touch has the power to instantly calm, reassure, transfer courage, and stabilize a situation beginning to spin out of control. With touch, we push back the threatening shadows of anger, bitterness, loneliness, and insecurity. Romantic touching and hugging can convey peace and comfort, as well as love. To the degree that we employ it with our mate, we remove the emotional threats that block intimacy.

Men nurture a forever marriage by finding out how their wives like to be touched, how often, when, and where.

Meaningful touching outside the bedroom can create sparks in a marriage, and meaningful communication can fan the flames. Most women report that they *need* to feel emotionally connected to enjoy physical intimacy. They need to feel loved and cherished. They need displays of physical affection, but not necessarily the sex act itself. Men, however, are motivated by the sexual act. They *need* sexual intimacy and state that physical affection and feeling cherished aren't always necessary for them to feel sexually satisfied. However, men still need affection and cherishing in the overall relationship.

These are the four elements of marital intimacy:

- *Unconditional security,* a lifetime commitment to care for someone.

- *Meaningful communication,* daily sharing your feelings, needs, hopes, and dreams (and being a good listener when the other person speaks).

- *Romantic experiences,* setting your schedule to include intimate times together rather than letting the pressures of life set your schedule for you.

- *Intimate touch,* since 8 to 10 loving touches a day keep the marriage counselor away!

When used correctly, the differences in the way men and women respond to sex can complement each other. When not taken into consideration, these differences will tear apart the very fabric of your mutual fulfillment. Decide to stop waiting for things to get better. Only the two of you working together toward love will make the intimate difference. Acquire and practice new attitudes and skills that lead to fulfilling relationships.

*Song of Solomon 2:4*

## Choosing Love or Anger

We choose our actions and responses every hour of every day. Sort the following acts and attitudes into those that express either love or anger, and then add some of your own thoughts:

- Compare and criticize the apparent flaws of your spouse to others.
- Gently place your arm around your spouse.
- Sit close to each other even when just watching television.
- Use humor to demean and belittle your spouse when talking.
- Argue in front of others so as to avoid a more heated debate.
- Make eye contact when your spouse is speaking.
- Give each other love notes to express your love in tangible ways.
- Take time to laugh together and lift each other with humor.
- Keep your needs from each other to create a sensual tension.
- Saying you're "sorry" first is a sign of weakness.

And over all these virtues put on love, which binds them all together in perfect unity.

~ Colossians 3:14

A gentle answer turns away wrath, but a harsh word stirs up anger.

~ Proverbs 15:1

# For the Husband

Answer the following questions and take some time to share the responses with your wife.

What is real intimacy? _____

_____

_____

_____

_____

How do you achieve romance or security in your marriage? _____

_____

_____

_____

_____

What will you do today to make your wife feel safe and secure in your affections?_____

_____

_____

_____

_____

*Principle step for the day:* Promise yourself to tell your wife daily what you appreciate about her. Encouraging notes or special gifts lift the spirit. Praise her in a way you know she'll enjoy.

# For the Wife

Answer the following questions and take some time to share the responses with your husband.

What is one thing you can do to increase the intimacy of your marriage?

_____

_____

_____

_____

How do you affirm your husband in your relationship?_____

_____

_____

_____

_____

What will you do today to make your husband feel safe and secure in your affections?_____

_____

_____

_____

_____

63

*Principle step for the day:* Touch has the power to instantly calm, reassure, transfer courage, and stabilize a situation beginning to spin out of control. Gently touch your husband through the day and you'll push back those shadows of anger, bitterness, and insecurity.

# 4 Trials and Treasures

Day 4

**treas·ure**

*-noun*

something or someone
highly valued

# Finding Treasures in Trials

**Gary:** One of the most helpful life skills
I've ever learned is what I call treasure-hunting
trials or finding treasures in trials. The concept
is simple, though doing it can be hard, especially
at first. But once you've made a habit
of it, the benefits are incredible. In
a nutshell, the idea is that even in
trying times and circumstances,
we can find some redeeming
good if we'll just look for it. No
matter how bad a situation may
be, there's something worthwhile
to be discovered. This concept
has been enormously helpful not
only to Norma and me, but it has also
helped—in some cases revolutionized
the lives of—many people with whom I've
counseled.

*Humble yourselves, therefore, under
God's mighty hand, that he may lift
you up in due time. Cast all your anxiety on him because he cares for you.*

*1 Peter 5:6–7*

**Norma:** Since learning how to do this,
treasure-hunting trials has become an emotional and spiritual life raft for me. For example,
when Gary does something to offend me (often
without even realizing it) and doesn't seek my
forgiveness, it's easy for me to feel hurt and
discouraged. When that happens, however, I've
learned to deal with it, with the Lord's help. First,
I take a few minutes to thank Him for Gary and for
the situation. I can do that sincerely—even though
I don't *feel* thankful yet—because I know God put
us together. I also know from experience that Gary's
intentions toward me are basically good and honoring. Second, because I'm confident that I *will* be able
to find good in the circumstance if I just look for
it, I ask myself, "What's one neat thing I'm learning because of the situation I'm in?" When I
take the time to think that way and do a little
digging, I always do find *at least* one good thing

65

in that trial. The treasure I find may be patience, greater compassion for others, a better understanding of how to get along with Gary, or something else. But whatever it is, it's always an insight or a strength that I'm glad to have in my life. On those rare occasions when Gary is down emotionally because of a difficulty, I'm even able to help him sometimes by getting him started on his own treasure-hunting.

**Gary:** I remember a time not long ago when I was really bothered by something and treasure-hunting again proved to be a great help. There's a strong history of heart trouble among the men in my family—both my father and a brother died relatively young of heart attacks. For a long time, I ignored the implications of that for myself. I didn't exercise, and I ate whatever I wanted, whenever I wanted it. Finally, a few years ago a doctor convinced me that I had to start taking better care of myself, and I became a "convert" to regular exercise and healthful eating.

Well, when I learn something or become convinced of something, I want everyone else to get on board as well! So when I became more health-conscious, I also thought Norma should start taking better care of *herself*—exercising, eating right, drinking lots of water, and so on.

**Norma:** When Gary does something like this, he becomes a fanatic! In front of a seminar audience, he comes across as highly motivating about whatever he believes in. But at home, he can be pushy and controlling. That makes me want to *resist* rather than get on board with him.

**Gary:** That's exactly what happened in this case. I didn't think she was as concerned about her health as she should be, so I started pushing, and she immediately started resisting. It became a point of contention and argument between us. This went on for several years, and I prayed about it every day. (Mostly I prayed that God would change Norma's mind.) Finally, although I was still concerned that she wasn't taking very good care of herself, I realized that my badgering wasn't doing any good, so I made a commitment to stop trying to "motivate" her. I decided I would leave the matter of how she cared for herself physically to her and God. I thought of this as a trial because I was as concerned about her as ever, and she wasn't doing any of the things yet that I thought she should. So I asked the Lord, "Where's the treasure in this, God? What good *has* come or *will* come out of this situation?" To my surprise, not long after I made that commitment, Norma started doing some of what I had hoped for all along to take better care of herself! For example, she started drinking a lot more water, which is a simple yet very healthful thing to do.

**Norma:** When Gary quit trying to be the Holy Spirit in my life in that area, telling me what I should and shouldn't do, I quit resisting. I actually gave some thought to what he had been saying for years, and I realized I could do some good things for myself without making radical changes in my lifestyle.

**Gary:** Out of that whole experience, I actually got two unexpected treasures. First, of course, Norma started doing some of the things that make for better health. That's a treasure to me not because she was finally doing what I wanted her to do, but because I want to enjoy her company for as long as possible, and her new habits should help to increase that time. Second, I got the treasure of watching *God* work things out that I never could have made happen myself. And in the process, I developed a greater trust in Him and in the power of prayer. Now, that's a treasure worth cherishing!

*Love is hidden in the pain. Practice thanking God during difficult circumstances.*

## Together in the Trials

No one likes trials, yet no one can escape them. We can let them ruin our lives—making us bitter, angry, and resentful—or we can look for the treasure that will let us love and serve others.

*1 John 4:18*

We'll catch the true meaning of Christ's teaching on faith if we pay attention to how He helped distraught people through their trials. Many of us make the mistake of forgetting that Jesus promises to produce maturity, righteousness, and love by letting us go through trials.

God's best and highest will is for us to love (value) Him with all our hearts, and to love (value) others as ourselves. Do you realize you have everything you need to fulfill God's will and experience His best in your life?

Almost every trial increases
our love for others. Even if
we don't see any other good,
we know of at least one—
more love.

Whenever I feel fear or worry, I thank the Lord for the feeling, and then test the following six reasons until I understand the source: the future, my reputation, money, possessions, time, or health. After that, I submit the concern to Him. Anger, hurt feelings, fear, and lust can actually help us develop a closer, more vital relationship with Jesus by serving as warning signals.

Keep a watchful eye on your mate's responses during a trial. During difficult times, it's vital not to do or say anything that will close the spirit of your spouse. Harsh words and callous actions in the heat of battle are the quickest way to dilute the "glue" of bonding. A few days after a trial, look for an opportunity

*The real secret to becoming a close-knit couple is shared experiences that turn into shared trials.*

to discuss how God could use it in his or her life.

Great faith is the confidence even *during* a trial that it will one day turn out to be to our benefit. "Dinky" faith is complaining or "murmuring" during a trial that there will be no benefit. Being neck-deep in a crisis doesn't find us saying, "Isn't this great?" Normally it gets tense, and we choke back words of anger and frustration. The secret is how we'll feel later. In most cases, it takes a couple of weeks for the "glue" of a shared predicament to set in place.

Disappointed expectations confront us all. *How we handle those disappointments will have a powerful impact on the peace and stability of our lives.* When we're hit with one of life's trials, we often overreact and panic. Before you tell yourself that this is a major disaster, take a few minutes to figure out what has transpired, assessing the actual damage. Remember, nothing is ever as bad as it seems at first glance. Though trouble may look at the time as if it's destroying your home, it can actually turn into a benefit through God's power!

Avoid the *blame* game. Don't allow guilt to overwhelm you when you notice negative emotional signals flashing. Rather, make a decision to use those signals as a motivation to evaluate and change your focus. Don't beat yourself up over mistakes you've made or personal losses or mistreatment you might have received. If you can avoid shame and blame, your recovery will be much quicker.

Allow yourself to grieve over any pain from discomforting experiences. Though I urge you to keep an optimistic outlook when confronted with a negative experience, it's still important to allow yourself to figure out what took place, analyze how it makes you feel, and sense the pain associated with the event. If you don't take this step, you can fall into denial and stuff the feelings so deep that you think you've solved the problem.

Whenever we're hit with a trial, if we don't allow ourselves to become angry and bitter, we'll become much more empathetic toward others who are experiencing similar problems and more sensitive to their feelings. All these things make us more loving and a better friend. The pain we feel for others helps us move forward in our personal journey into maturity. Additional benefits include heightened thoughtfulness, gentleness, carefulness, kindness, patience, and self-control.

69

Proverbs 10:12

# The Daily Treasure Hunt

Treasure hunting (looking for gold in every trial or guilt experience) can help us form a genuine love or deeper sensitivity toward others who are hurting in a similar way. It can also help us forgive those who have wronged us and cause us to be less judgmental or critical, leading us to the door of God's grace.

Sometimes the treasure is coated with corrosion, but if we do some scraping, we begin to see its value. Thanksgiving expresses our faith that God can, indeed, bring treasures out of trials, and faith adds muscle to the scraping process, even in the worst of trials. Every problem—great or small—has in it a treasure waiting to be discovered. The secret to successful treasure hunting is understanding two life-changing words: *faith* and *love*.

Life's game plan includes some changes you can anticipate and plan on. But it will also be filled with sneaky speed bumps, strange detours, frustrating dead ends, sudden lane changes, and unscheduled exits. If you anticipate both the major "expected" changes as well as probable unexpected changes, you'll stand a better chance of reaching your destination . . . together.

Avoid continual concentration on what you're losing or being denied in a trial. Try to think of what new opportunities this situation may bring, what you might learn from this obstacle, and what future happiness lies in store. Begin to treasure hunt as soon as possible and as long as you're able. This isn't something you do for just a short time after a trial; you continue doing it until your thinking actually changes and you realize the positive results of your positive thinking. You'll have a victory over your pain when you see the benefits of the event and have feelings of greater love and self-worth.

One method I use to discover the treasure in my personal trials is to write on a piece of paper a list of my past trials and what possible benefits have come from each of them. In the midst of our trials, God has designed a number of "home lightening" options that will bring warmth, brilliance, and beauty into our family rooms, dining rooms, bedrooms, and playrooms—bright lamps like unconditional affirmation, meaningful touch, hard-earned wisdom, unquestioned character, and spiritual dependence on Him.

Finding benefits in a trial may not come until months after it's over. But when you feel you can, here are some elements that can be discovered within any negative situation:

*Self-appreciation.* List things you like about yourself.

*Support system.* List the people who have helped you through your more serious trials.

*Increased love.* List the ways the trial has helped you understand and care about others.

When you begin to treasure hunt *past* trials in your life, you'll develop a greater freedom from the pain that may still be affecting you. Anger will begin to evaporate, and areas of intimacy will open up.

Steps involved in treasure hunting:

1. Recognize the pain you've experienced—don't deny the anger and hurt.

2. When it's called for, go through a grieving period.

3. During the midst of a trial, hang on to the hand of God. Concentrate on keeping your eyes and expectations focused on Him.

4. Wait expectantly on the Lord, like a child on Christmas morning, to bring to light the gold, blessing, or benefits that come from the trials you're experiencing.

5. Use the extra sensitivity, compassion, endurance, or wisdom you've gained from a trial to help others.

Whenever you begin to feel fear or worry, thank the Lord for the feeling. Then look at what might be causing it. Is it related to your future expectations? Is it your reputation? If you know which area has caused the fear or worry, present that to God as a confession of your need to trust Him to take care of the results.

Three thoughts will help anyone facing a major transition in life: Let go, start fresh, and reach out.

## God in the Middle

**Gary:** The key to a satisfying marriage is most likely to occur when we put God at the center of the relationship and commit our lives to Him, both individually and as a couple. One of the ways we do that, as I mentioned earlier, is that Norma and I pray together about anything and everything that looks difficult or challenging in our relationship, our family, or our ministry. In doing so we acknowledge that He's our Lord, that we need His guidance, and that without His strength we won't succeed. We also honor Him in that we never give up hope that He can fix whatever's wrong in our marriage (or any other area of need)—that He can do something supernatural to work things together for good. We know that He, in turn, will honor His Word in James 1:5–6 and give us the wisdom we need when we ask for it in faith.

*James 1:5-6*

**Norma:** I remember a time, many years ago, when I had to make a very difficult choice if I was going to honor God in our marriage. Our finances were in deep trouble then, and I was the family bookkeeper and bill payer. Gary was not the most responsible person in handling money, so I really didn't trust him in that area. Then I heard a message in which the speaker said the husband ought to handle a couple's finances, and I was convicted by it. Now, neither Gary nor I necessarily agree that the husband should *always* handle the finances, and we don't believe the Bible teaches it. Generally, whichever spouse is best at doing it should have the job. And today, I manage that area for both our family and our ministry. At that time, however, the issue before me wasn't which of us could handle the checkbook better. It was, "Since I believe God is asking me to give this area over to Gary as a matter of obedience to Him, do I trust Him enough to do it? I can't trust Gary at this point, but will I trust God?"

**Gary:** When Norma says I wasn't responsible back then, she's putting the case charitably. From a logical perspective, it made no sense to hand our financial affairs over to me. Apart from God's intervention, she had every reason to expect that obeying Him would lead to disaster.

**Norma:** In spite of the danger, however, I was convinced that this was what God wanted me to do. And so it became a simple matter: did I trust Him, and would I obey Him? It wasn't an easy choice, but finally I decided that I did and I would. I'm happy to report that God did intervene, and Gary grew tremendously in his ability to handle our finances responsibly. It didn't happen overnight, and that can be a difficult thing, because we tend to want God to make everything better right away. But over a period of many months, Gary "grew up" far more than I could have even hoped and became extremely responsible, to the point where I really could trust him in this area. Today, when I tell this story to an audience, women will come to me afterward and say, "I couldn't do what you did." But to my mind, it was a matter of honoring God and obeying Him when I sensed His clear direction. So my question to those women, and to you who are reading this book, is simply this: how much do you trust God?

**Gary:** Our purpose here isn't to preach at anyone. But we will say that in our experience, we have never been disappointed when we've put our trust in God. And our marriage is much the stronger as a result. We've been together for more than 40 years now, and the "dance" keeps getting better every day. We pray the same will be true for you and your mate.

Psalm 119:168

# Toward the Overflowing Life

Galatians 2:20

God's Word contains the only genuine blueprint for successful relationships, both with Him and with others.

As I seek God daily, making sure I have His desires and believe Him for those desires, I can be assured of one thing— He answers the persistent prayers of His children. This is as true for our marriages as it is for any other area of life. God truly modeled the principles of touching when Jesus walked the back trails and highways of planet Earth. No longer could God be thought of as some distant, unconcerned deity in a far corner of infinity. He came, robed in warm, human flesh. And while He walked among us, He reached out His hands.

Many husbands and wives put their hopes for fulfillment in people or in places, whether homes or vacation spots. To those thirsting for fulfillment, these things look like a quenching pool of water. Yet once they reach them, they find only the sand of a mirage. Only Christ gives everlasting satisfaction.

Probably the most important thing that negative emotions reveal is our own self-centeredness. We need to admit our level of self-centeredness, because out of such an admission comes the freedom to refocus our expectations away from God's creation and onto God Himself. We live overflowing lives because the *source* of life, instead of the *gifts* (people, places, possessions, and position) of life, brings us contentment. How? By leading us to the well that never runs dry.

> When Christ is in control, our negative emotions are replaced by an inner contentment and love that come only from Him.

Transfer the ownership and authority of your life, including your marriage, to God (see Galatians 2:20). Establish God's Word and the leading of the Holy Spirit as your final authority (see Psalm 19:11). Expect God, through Christ, to meet all your needs (see Philippians 4:19).

When we rejoice in the Lord always, He keeps us, in many situations, from giving in to such temptations as envy, jealousy, fear, and anger. Rejoicing, even in times of testing, is acknowledging that God is the source of life. And it brings us to the place where our lives can be filled by God Himself.

# The Character Builder

If your focus strays from depending on Christ for strength and creativity, you may find yourself nagging your spouse. Anger and nagging usually stem from feelings of frustration at failing to change another person. While these "helpful reminders" may come from a sincere desire to help, actually they *demotivate* a person and are a constant weight on him or her. Depending on God to change another person, rather than on ourselves, can have powerful results in a relationship.

God's grace is power in us to control our tongue, even in heated discussions with a spouse, but He only gives grace to the humble. If we humble ourselves in His presence, recognizing our complete dependence on Him, He will exalt us.

Whatever your goals and ambitions for improving your marriage, you must learn the necessary skills, even though it may take years. Don't limit yourself and God by dwelling on what you already know and can do. God has established spiritual laws, or principles, in all relationships, especially marriage. It's our responsibility to discover these principles, measure our lives by them, and correct any behavior that is "off center" from God's best.

> People, places, and things will never make you happy. Happiness comes from within.

The "quest for success" comes with a high price tag. Many women and men spend years of their lives climbing the ladder of success—only to find when they reach the top that the ladder is leaning against the wrong wall. Status and titles do little to light up our lives—they can never take the places of family and God. Did you ever count on the road of life and marriage being as rough as it turned out to be? It happens. But maybe you also never counted on a Friend who loves you as much as God does. For He Himself said, "I will never leave you nor forsake you" (Joshua 1:5).

75

Joshua 1:5

God wants us to be mature, loving people who reflect Jesus Christ's character in every area of life, including marriage. The only way He can make that happen is to allow trials. It's important to note that God doesn't *cause* the trials. They come from many sources, including our own sinful nature and Satan, God's enemy. But God uses them for our ultimate benefit.

We honor God by serving Him. Seeing people (like our mate) renewed, healed, blessed, encouraged, and motivated by our love for them increases our self-worth as servants of God. Learning what your spouse needs and looking for creative ways to meet those needs unlocks the door of serving. Genuine fulfillment comes through knowing and loving God first, and then through serving others in response to His love.

We dishonor God when we live with an attitude of ungratefulness. We know we're ungrateful when we are constantly comparing what we have with the possessions or positions (or marriages) of others; continually complaining about the way "life" is treating us; always fearful; trying to manipulate others; and so on.

Important Biblical Convictions in Marriage

| | |
|---|---|
| Having a loving relationship with my spouse and children | Ephesians 5:21–33 |
| Spending quality time alone with my spouse and together with my family | Following Christ's example of being alone with His disciples Mark 4:10–20 |
| Not allowing unresolved hurts to come between us; being tenderhearted and forgiving each other | Ephesians 4:32 |
| Honoring, or "blessing," each other | Ephesians 5:33, 1 Peter 3:7 |
| Expressing appreciation and minimizing a critical attitude toward each other | 1 Corinthians 13:5–6 |
| Endeavoring to be united in mind, spirit, and flesh | Ephesians 5:31 Philippians 1:27; 2:2–3 |
| Being committed to care unconditionally for my family | 1 Timothy 5:8, Genesis 2:24 |

Ungratefulness. Trace it to the failure to find benefits in everything & a reluctance to trust God to fulfill our needs.

## Choosing Love or Anger

We choose our actions and responses every hour of every day. Circle Yes or No in the following questions and score yourself to see if you tend to choose love or anger in various situations:

I usually remain calm even if someone completely disagrees with me. (Yes = love / No = anger)

There has never been a time when I have struck or pushed someone even when upset. (Yes = love / No = anger)

People generally try and avoid arguing with me because I am highly competitive. (Yes = anger / No = love)

Most would say they have rarely, if ever heard me raise my voice in an argument. (Yes = love / No = anger)

There have been times when I have broken things because my emotions got carried away in a fight. (Yes = anger / No = love)

Often if I have to wait or I feel that I am being insulted I can begin to lose my temper. (Yes = anger / No = love)

When a disagreement is resolved, I try to never bring it up in the future and use the information against my spouse. (Yes = love / No = anger)

I really do love a good argument, showing other people how much I know. (Yes = anger / No = love)

It is vital that responsibility for a problem be discovered so blame can be placed. (Yes = anger / No = love)

Ultimately, issues will come and go; what is most important is making sure my spouse feels safe and secure with me no matter the situation. (Yes = love / No = anger)

LOVE _____ ANGER _____

Proverbs 29:22

# For the Husband

Write down and discuss with your spouse a few of the thoughts that face you in that "aha" moment.

Finding Treasure in Trials _____

_____

_____

_____

_____

God in the Middle _____

_____

_____

_____

_____

Why is honoring God so important for a couple?_____

_____

_____

_____

_____

*Principle step for the day:* Focus on all you are grateful for no matter the outcome of the day. Treasure hunting is transforming bitter into better. When you're bitter, you're angry and feel low self-worth. When you're better, you feel appreciative and can better meet your wife's needs.

# For the Wife

Write down and discuss with your spouse a few of the thoughts that face you in that "aha" moment

Finding Treasure in Trials _____

_____

_____

_____

_____

God in the Middle _____

_____

_____

_____

_____

Why is honoring God so important for a couple?_____

_____

_____

_____

_____

*Principle step for the day:* Focus on trusting God to meet all your needs. This will allow you to take the focus off your own needs, and refocus your efforts on meeting your husband's needs, helping him in areas of struggle.

# From This Day Forth

You've finished the main portion of this four-day challenge, and now we hope that you'll maintain the loving momentum by remembering that love is a choice, not simply a feeling. Each day commit to choosing love, not anger.

Remember those questions at the beginning of the book? Here they are again for you to review and discuss to see if your responses might have changed or if in talking these through you can both come to a deeper understanding of each other.

1. What does a good relationship look like to you?
2. What hinders a good relationship?
3. Where is our relationship today on a scale of 1 to 10?
4. What would it take to make our relationship better?

When things in life get rough, and they will, hold onto that hope that every trial has a treasure inside of it. Reflect often on these three principles:

1. Trials will come daily and they will make me better or bitter. I will choose to have them make me better.
2. I will say to the Lord, "Thank You." He did not say I had to feel thankful, but to express it either way.
3. I will look for that pearl or treasure every day. I do believe that each trial has one for me.

Copy these and put them in your purse or wallet, or up on the fridge. And remember to choose love from this day forth....

'For this reason a man will leave his father and mother and be united to his wife, and the two will become one flesh.' So they are no longer two, but one. Therefore what God has joined together, let man not separate."
Mark 10:7-9

Marriage is hard. The day we said "I do" it was a commitment to the Lord, and we knew it was forever. To us that is so big, and we had no idea how much work and how hard it would be. We are so different from each other, so it was that commitment to the Lord, that vow that has made the difference; it helped us hang in there when things got hard. We wonder how many couples reading this book may even now need to make that commitment to the Lord.

Many countless blessings on your life today and from this day forth.... *Gary & Norma*

# Your Season of Marriage

Engaged Couples                    Newly Married Couples

Ecclesiastes 3:1

83

Married with Children    Empty Nesters / Remarriage

## Engaged Couples: The Best is Yet to Come

Norma was so cooperative before we got married; I thought she would be submissive. I was self-centered. Expectations you have about the one you are to marry can create great frustration if they are unrealistic. The more you get to know the one you love, the closer to reality your expectations become, and the more satisfied you can be with your life together.

Take time to get to know each other's character, dreams, even weaknesses. As a couple, you will be there for each other through blessings and trials, and must be able to forgive faults, as you will discover that no one is perfect. Trust that things, no matter how difficult, can and will get better.

Cultivate times weekly when you can communicate on a deeper level than mere events and facts; times when you get to the heart of what each of you feel and need. In the security of each other, take the risk to ask: "What are you feeling right now?" As you are learning to know each other better, take a moment to clarify in your own words whether or not you understood the message and the motive.

Look for ways to bless and honor the one you love. When your energy is spent trying to manipulate him or her to please you, demanding your own way, this can only create an atmosphere of pain and frustration. You must allow God to meet your deepest needs, and not expect this of your husband- or wife-to-be.

Your relationship can be deeply strengthened as you learn to appreciate your differences as well as your similarities. And those differences are beautiful in God's eyes. God looks at the differences between all of us and finds joy because He made us and created us. He has given each of us a unique blend of gifts, talents, strengths, and weaknesses. If you can see these unique traits as simply diverse ways of approaching life, rather than faults or stupid mistakes, you'll find a balance in a relationship that gives and takes. If you always insist that your opinion or view is the correct one, you may eventually alienate your partner and make him or her feel devalued. Take time to ask: "How can our differences draw us together?"

Find ways each day to communicate love and praise. Words can bring such blessing and strength to the one you love, whether the words are spoken or written.

Additional resources from Gary Smalley:

- *As Long as We Both Shall Live,* with Ted Cunningham (Regal, 2009).
- *If Only He Knew,* with Norma Smalley (Zondervan, 1997).
- *For Better or for Best* (Zondervan, 2011).
- *I Promise You Forever* (Thomas Nelson, 2007).
- *Making Love Last Forever* (Thomas Nelson, 1997).

Two are better than one, because they have a good return for their labor.

Ecclesiastes 4:9

## Newly Married Couples: After the Honeymoon

Do you want to know the deep satisfaction that comes from being in love? It's simple. It's your choice. You must choose daily between love or anger. Adjusting to your new life together can take time, and can create unexpected frustrations, so recognizing what creates an environment of anger and choosing love and honor instead will help establish a sound, safe environment.

When you are offended by your spouse, try to understand the "why" behind the hurtful action. In this way you can let love cover over the response, rather than reacting with hurt as well.

It is vital for new couples to make their home a secure place where neither partner feels belittled or devalued. As a crisis arises, you work together as a team to resolve the issues and move forward united even stronger.

Find time periodically to sit down and ask the question: "What would make our relationship better?" Agree together beforehand that this will be done in a positive way, and not a defensive way that points out faults or mistakes you feel your spouse might have made. Look for ways to make attitudes, actions, and the whole atmosphere of the home better. Make sure that you implement at least some of your suggestions within the next week.

There will be times you'll need to share things with your spouse that he or she has done, knowingly or unknowingly, that may have hurt you. Make sure your praise far outweighs negative statements by at least seven to one. Also, know that love will not make impossible demands but is willing to look at things realistically.

Build positive connections with other married couples in order to have some accountability, and to develop support for each other's marriages. Sometimes it can be beneficial to see relationships through another set of lenses, and to welcome a fresh perspective and insight from those who can perhaps be more objective about your situation.

Additional resources from Gary Smalley:

- *The DNA of Relationships*, (Tyndale House Publishers, 2007).
- *Joy that Lasts*, with Al Janssen (Zondervan, 2002).
- *Making Love Last Forever* (Thomas Nelson, 1997).
- *The Hidden Value of a Man*, with John Trent (Living Books, 2005).
- *From Anger to Intimacy: How Forgiveness Can Transform Your Marriage,* with Ted Cunningham (Regal, 2009).
- *The Language of Sex: Experiencing the Beauty of Sexual Intimacy,* with Ted Cunningham (Regal, 2008).

87

Therefore, as God's chosen people, holy and dearly loved, clothe yourselves with compassion, kindness, humility, gentleness and patience. Bear with each other and forgive one another if any of you has a grievance against someone. Forgive as the Lord forgave you. And over all these virtues put on love, which binds them all together in perfect unity.

Colossians 3:12–14

## Married with Children: Little Feet and Chips on the Couch

When your husband disciplines one of your children, avoid the temptation to criticize him in front of the child or defend the child's action that provoked his correction. The first step in developing a calm attitude is to control your tendency to overreact.

Wise parents will realize that each child has his or her own unique set of needs. The Book of Proverbs shows us this. Every child has varying temperaments, talents, and capacities that God has given to him or her. A parent should pay close attention to find how they might support each child's individual gifts.

*Proverbs 22:6*

It's wise to learn that marital conflict is inevitable, and this can be intensified when children are involved. Their tangible and genuine demands and needs can distract parents from their own marital needs. Take time to get away by yourselves, even if just for a walk. This alone can show your spouse that his or her needs are important enough that you want to focus on your relationship with no interruptions.

When parents fail to say no, unwanted attitudes are allowed to take root in their homes. This builds learned helplessness and irresponsibility within kids. Such parents should be charged with delinquency of a minor.

We need to find a better way to communicate a message of high value and acceptance, a way to picture a person's valuable qualities and traits apart from his or her performance. Words have incredible power to build us up or tear us down emotionally. This is particularly true when it comes to giving or gaining family approval.

Make time to be alone together, connecting on four levels: verbally, emotionally, physically, and spiritually. Children will eventually leave the home, and your relationship will thrive in your next season (empty nest) of marriage if you made each other the priority the entire time. This will leave a powerful example for your grown kids as well, as they remember the loving model you lived out for them.

Additional resources from Gary Smalley:

- *The Blessing: Giving the Gift of Unconditional Love and Acceptance*, with John Trent (Thomas Nelson, 2011)
- *The DNA of Parent-Teen Relationships*, with Greg Smalley (Tyndale House Publishers, 2005)
- *Great Parents, Lousy Lovers*, with Ted Cunningham (Tyndale House Publishers, 2010).
- *Guarding Your Child's Heart* (NavPress, 2010).
- *The Key to Your Child's Heart* (Thomas Nelson, 1983).

89

Children are a heritage from the Lord,
offspring a reward from him.
Like arrows in the hands of a warrior
are children born in one's youth.

—Psalm 127:3–4

# Empty Nesters: Redefining Who and What You Are

A lonesome feeling can arise once all the children have left home, leaving a couple sitting in silence if they have not maintained their own relationship while the kids were home. Take this time to get to know each other better, and celebrate it as a second courtship.

Lives can drift apart if not lived intentionally and purposefully. Make a concerted effort each day to share tender touches and gentle words of encouragement, and each week set aside times to reconnect as a couple.

Joy can come through being able to keep your friendship established with your adult children, and your influence can grow as they seek your guidance. Also, grandparents love to share their wisdom, but they have to earn the respect to share advice not just give it.

Grandparents are actually raising their grandchildren at times. They need to be able to set boundaries to support and guide, but not to parent. Connect every day to your grand-kids by praying over their pictures, encouraging their hopes and dreams, and finding ways through traditional and new media sources to help them sense your love.

You want the best for your grand-kids, but you have to remind yourself not to go overboard. You are the grandparent, and you must restrain yourself. Relationships always have to be developed and strengthened...

always. Some conflicts arise when healthy boundaries haven't been set. Talk these over with the parents, and support their rules; know what they expect. If a parent says no, then teach your grandchild to honor his or her parents.

You can build a legacy of love in your grandchildren when you take time to learn more about their lives and individual struggles. If a grandparent maintains a loving and caring relationship with his or her grandkids, it's so much easier to share truths with them.

Don't let these days just slip away from you or expect your lives to adjust without an effort from you and your spouse. Make sure you talk about the day's events, as well as your feelings and dreams for the days and years ahead.

Take time to go on walks and dinner dates, as well as connect with other couples. These can be joyful times of reflection, sharing thoughts of the past, as well as making new memories with caring, supportive friends.

Additional resources from Gary Smalley:

- *The Blessing: Giving the Gift of Unconditional Love and Acceptance*, with John Trent (Thomas Nelson, 2011).

- *I Promise: How 5 Essential Commitments Determine the Destiny of Your Marriage* (Thomas Nelson, 2006).

91

Only be careful, and watch yourselves closely so that you do not forget the things your eyes have seen or let them fade from your heart as long as you live. Teach them to your children and to their children after them.

Deuteronomy 4:9

## Remarriage: Blending Two Worlds

Remember there are adjustments in remarriage, especially if there are children from a previous marriage. Whether you have remarried after being divorced or widowed, there will be dramatic changes as you learn the routines, habits, and likes and dislikes of another, and yet still have a connection to the previous marriage. Focus on your spouse first, and the needs of the children second. Not that your children aren't just as important, but it's the husband and wife who become one.

Know that even small behavioral changes can bring about major improvements in relationships. Keep these in mind when working through adjustments in schedules and life situations. Simply developing a heart of nurturing can draw you and your spouse closer together. This includes making sure he or she feels safe to be who he or she are, maintaining meaningful times of conversation, creating emotional and romantic moments, and using consistent, positive physical touches.

Take full responsibility for your choices, and know that meaningful communication takes time. You have to make an effort to focus on the needs of your new spouse, and to build the rapport that will strengthen your relationship, making your home the safe haven it needs to be.

If you have certain expectations of your spouse, discuss these and let him or her do the same. They may be reasonable and supportive ideas, or they may be irrational or even destructive to your new relationship. Remember that love allows others to think for themselves, encouraging conversation and listening intently.

No person loves perfectly, and your spouse will most likely fail to love you the way you want at various times in your marriage. You must understand that no human can give you enough love to fulfill you. This being said, don't put pressure on your spouse to heal hurts that have been inflicted over the years, either when you were younger or in your previous marriage. Only God can ultimately meet this need and bring you that deep sense of joy and peace that is boundless.

Additional resources:

- *The Blessing: Giving the Gift of Unconditional Love and Acceptance,* with John Trent (Thomas Nelson, 2011).
- *Great Parents, Lousy Lovers,* with Ted Cunningham (Tyndale House Publishers, 2010).

The Lord God said, "It is not good for the man to be alone. I will make a helper suitable for him."

Genesis 2:18

# Fulfilling a Legacy Through God-given Dreams

Hebrews 11:1

## Marriage and Mentoring the Next Generation

A book on marriage may seem an odd place to talk about dreams, but they are actually an important part of everyone. Our hopes and dreams not only define us; they are also the challenges that we put so much time and energy toward achieving. The investment of ourselves in our dreams will impact every relationship we may have, and if we are part of a marriage, together we share and work toward our individual and family dreams — and that can include our children or grandchildren as well. If you keep God at the center of your dreams, you can achieve anything!

Consider this: another word for dreams or dreaming is faith, because faith is the substance of things hoped for and the evidence of things we can't see yet (Hebrews 11:1). A dream is seeing something that hasn't come about yet. Now there are books about making your dreams reality, but often these are written from a secular standpoint; they leave out any aspect of glorifying God or having dreams in line with God's purpose. A dream like that can leave one empty and flat, like having a dream to win the lottery. So many of those people who win go bankrupt or lose touch with their families… some of the consequences of ungodly dreams. One must always ask God to reveal His dream for us, and our prayers can be a powerful way to align our heart's dream with God's plan for our life.

Over 30 years ago, I believed that God had given me five dreams that He wanted me to fulfill in order to love others:

1. Write a book
2. Develop and preach ten messages on marriage and family
3. Make movies and videos
4. Speak at conferences
5. Stay connected to reality by continually counseling couples and families.

I had struggled in school because of a poor reading level, so writing a book seemed an impossible dream. Though I had no reason to think writing a book would ever be a real possibility, I learned that grades or abilities aren't the most important factor, but knowing that Christ can work through you no matter what. We must be humbled for His will. Do you have ADHD or dyslexia? Well, it ultimately doesn't matter; nothing is impossible for God. Your dreams can be fulfilled through Christ!

I already had grown to know that God's main will for each person who is following His Son's commands is to love God with all of his or her heart, soul, mind, and strength, and to love and care for others in the same way he or she loves him or herself. I used 1 Timothy 6:2b–5 to discover what specifically God wanted me to do in loving Him and others.

1 Timothy 6:2b–5

("These are the things you are to teach and insist on. If anyone teaches otherwise and does not agree to the sound instruction of our Lord Jesus Christ and to godly teaching, they are conceited and understand nothing. They have an unhealthy interest in controversies and quarrels about words that result in envy, strife, malicious talk, evil suspicions and constant friction between people of corrupt mind, who have been robbed of the truth and who think that godliness is a means to financial gain.") That verse directed me to make sure that all of my doctrine aligned with two instructions:

1. Is what I'm thinking of doing to serve God consistent with what Christ said?
2. Would what I want to do in loving Him and others lead them and me to godliness?

95

An open willingness to obey God's direction in our lives can be so powerful, if we are willing to release the control we feel we have to have, and lay our dreams at the feet of God. He is at work in our lives leading us to our purpose, even when we are blind to the dream unfolding before us.

As I mentioned, God had placed a five-part dream on my heart. Prior to this, I had been really knocked down on my job; some really bad stuff happened, even in a Christian office. I quit, broken and hurt and frustrated, and didn't know what to do. We moved away and I took an assistant pastor's job, but was just drained and unable to forgive. Beauty came from the ashes of my life, and when I forgave there was such a release. I started praying every day, and felt called to family ministry — again, God's plan at work in my life. In just two years all five dreams — once so seemingly impossible — came to fruition.

## Following God's Lead

I strongly felt lead to strengthen marriages and families, and it was confirmed by several people in my church. I waited until God gave me amazing peace about this direction, according to the passage in 1 Timothy. After seeking counsel from my church elders and receiving their blessing and the church's calling to minister to those who were married and raising families, I set out to find the Lord's leading with what specifically He wanted me to do.

I knew that I would not be able to fulfill any of my new dreams without Him opening the doors. I could try to "force" a door open to get one of them, but I knew from the past that it's a lot better if I just wait for Him to do it. I constantly kept "crying out to my God" daily, and I didn't start calling people, emailing them, or begging anyone to help me open doors for the dreams He gave me. Only He knows exactly when doors will open. All I did was wake up each morning with the dreams He had given me and imagine that "today is the day that one or all of them will happen."

You know that God is faithful to His children who come to Him each day, crying out for a miracle from Him to open the door to the dreams He has given us. Here's what I did each day:

1. Continually checked with 1 Timothy 6:2b–5 to see if what I felt called to do was consistent with Christ's words and will; what He has placed in my heart to lead others and myself to godliness.

2. Meditated on Luke 11 and 18, two parables on persistent prayer. One is of the hungry man knocking on the door for a miracle, and the other of the little old widow woman, crying out to the wicked judge for protection.

These experiences had a profound effect on my life, ministry, and most importantly, my family. My grandkids know my story, and that nothing is impossible through Christ. This is why I keep asking my grandkids what God is laying on their hearts, and their dreams to love and serve others. Once they gain peace from God about what He is calling them to do, they can begin doing what I did and find God just as faithful to them as He was with me.

If you, then, though you are evil, know how to give good gifts to your children, how much more will your Father in heaven give good gifts to those who ask him! So in everything, do to others what you would have them do to you, for this sums up the Law and the Prophets.

Matthew 7:11–12

# Our Family Dreamboard

We came up with an incredible strategy for connecting with our grandchildren, keeping track of their dreams, and to remind us daily to keep these precious prayers within our own words with God. In the past, we have had a dream board of our grandchildren at the back door of our home. It is a beautiful way to help us keep connected to their lives, no matter how far away they might be. When we speak with them we inevitably ask them about their dreams or goals. We then write these down and post them with their picture on the board, taking time each day to lift them up in prayer.

It is unbelievably special to be reminded each time you look at or walk past the dreamboard how God is starting now to work in the lives of our grandchildren to be faithful representatives of Christ in whatever careers or missions they are led to undertake in the future. It is a powerful legacy of faith, a loving, committed marriage, and a strong family that is helping to shape their lives each day.

One of my granddaughters believes God has called her to become a pediatrician to serve kids as a missionary doctor. Another one dreams about being a singer and an actor to gain the platform to share the message of Christ's salvation. Our oldest grandson is so very unique. His life was revolutionized when I got him to memorize Scripture when he was 10. Now he's fearless. And he has such compassion and is helping to dig a well in Ethiopia where they have no clean water. On the wall is a dream for him; he wants to take over for Matt Lauer, and I have no doubt it will happen. Another granddaughter has a dream of becoming a pastry chef; God can really use that. She just needs to ask God for peace and then get ready… meet with the best… prepare for her dreams. One grandson wants to be a man of God, a pro golfer, and win the Master's. One granddaughter is praying for a godly husband and while she has not even started dating yet, she talks to me about marriage and is a true dreamer. And still another wants to be a professional singer and we found that someone in town trains young girls how to sing so she can begin to work toward her goal!

Michael
& Amy
Smalley
family

Roger
& Kari
Gibson
family

99

Greg
& Erin
Smalley
family

All ten grandkids love that they had their favorite dreams up on the wall; it makes them feel they're part of a team and constantly in our hearts…all part of the Smalley clan. I pray that when they grow up and help change the world for Christ, they continue this loving legacy of prayer and a dreamboard with their own families.

If you have children or grandchildren, make sure you interact with them as often as possible… by phone, email, Skype. All things are possible with God, and He cannot be unfaithful to His children. My grandkids know these verses and know the foundation of trusting in God daily for their lives, their dreams, and the great adventure of walking daily with God. His Word is a lamp unto our feet… Remind them of Scripture…. Rejoice in your trials… Show them how to seek their dreams… and pray daily for God's will within each one!

My dear brothers, take note of this: Everyone should be quick to listen, slow to speak and slow to become angry, for man's anger does not bring about the righteous life that God desires..

James 1:19–20

# Five Key Scriptures

Do not be anxious about anything, but in everything, by prayer and petition, with thanksgiving, present your requests to God.

And the peace of God, which transcends all understanding, will guard your hearts and your minds in Christ Jesus.

Finally, brothers, whatever is true, whatever is noble, whatever is right, whatever is pure, whatever is lovely, whatever is admirable — if anything is excellent or praiseworthy — think about such things.

Whatever you have learned or received or heard from me, or seen in me — put it into practice. And the God of peace will be with you.

Philippians 4:6–9

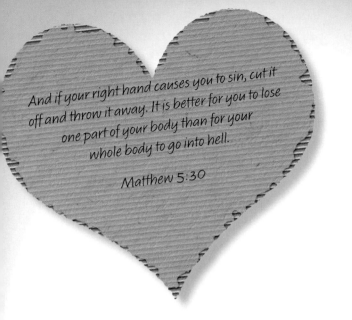

And if your right hand causes you to sin, cut it off and throw it away. It is better for you to lose one part of your body than for your whole body to go into hell.

Matthew 5:30

Anyone who claims to be in the light but hates his brother is still in the darkness.

Whoever loves his brother lives in the light, and there is nothing in him to make him stumble.

But whoever hates his brother is in the darkness and walks around in the darkness; he does not know where he is going, because the darkness has blinded him.

1 John 2:9–11

Not only so, but we also rejoice in our sufferings, because we know that suffering produces perseverance; perseverance, character; and character, hope. And hope does not disappoint us, because God has poured out his love into our hearts by the Holy Spirit, whom he has given us.

Romans 5:3–5

# The Smalley "Fighting Rules"

◌ First clarify what the actual conflict is. Make sure that you understand your partner as clearly as you can before proceeding to a resolution. Listening is vital here! Endeavor to work for understanding in two key areas: your mate's feelings and then needs.

◌ Stick to the issue at hand. Don't dredge up past hurts or problems, whether real or perceived. But if you tend to veer off the issue, you might want to see if there is any other key factor in this conflict, such as fatigue, low estrogen levels, low blood sugar, stress, work problems, or spiritual or emotional issues.

◌ Maintain as much tender physical contact as possible. Hold hands.

◌ Avoid sarcasm.

◌ Avoid "you" statements. Use the words "I feel" or "I think." No past or future predictions ("You always..." "You won't ever...").

◌ Don't use "hysterical" statements or exaggerations. ("This will never work out." "You're just like your father.")

◌ Resolve any hurt feelings before continuing the conflict discussion. ("I shouldn't have said that. Will you forgive me?")

◌ Don't resort to name-calling. Don't allow the conflict to escalate your tempers. If this happens, agree to continue the discussion later.

◌ Avoid power statements and actions. For example: "I quit!" "You sleep on the couch tonight!" "You're killing me!" "I hate you!"

◌ Don't use the silent treatment.

◌ Keep your arguments as private as possible to avoid embarrassment.

◌ Use the "drive-through" method of communication when arguing. (Repeat back what you think the other person is saying.)

◌ Resolve your conflicts with win-win solutions; both parties agree with the solution or outcome of the argument. Work on resolution only after both understand feelings and needs.

◌ Above all, strive to reflect honor in all your words and actions during the resolution of your conflicts.

(*Making Love Last Forever* [Thomas Nelson, 1997], pages 221–222)

# A Dozen Ways to Engage Your Spouse

1.  You're both home from work at the end of the day. Set aside a 15-minute period at some point to discuss (reflect on) your respective day's activities.

2.  Make a rule that the TV is off during dinner, encouraging conversation. For that hour, let the answering machine take all phone calls except emergencies.

3.  Write a monthly date night into your schedule that cannot be broken.

4.  If your schedule permits, get together for lunch once a week even if you're just brown-bagging it in the park.

5.  As a couple, attend one of your children's sports games or other performances. It's amazing how conversation can develop while you sit and watch your child or on the way to and from the game.

6.  Take a walk together after dinner. It's a good time to talk, and it's also good for you physically.

7.  If you are allowed some flexibility in your work schedule, go in late one day, after the kids have all gone off to school. Enjoy the hour with your spouse.

8.  Read a magazine article or book together that you both feel will stimulate a discussion.

9.  Don't be afraid to use baby sitters just to give you time alone to talk.

10. Write each other little notes that begin, "I have something really amazing to talk with you about the next time we're together."

11. Once or twice a year, plan a weekend getaway for just the two of you.

12. Ask your best friend to hold you accountable to meet with your mate at least once a week for a meaningful conversation.

103

(Remember that a certain sex killer is to combine a serious discussion about some conflictive issue while on a fun date, during an intimate talk, or just before or right after the sexual experience. Plan your conflict discussions during the week at a specific time and day.)

*(Making Love Last Forever* [Thomas Nelson, 1997], pages 238–239)

# Romance on a Shredded Shoestring Budget

1. Dress up for a meal you bring back from your favorite fast food restaurant.

2. Buy a half gallon of your favorite ice cream, go to the most beautiful park in town, throw a blanket on the ground, and eat the whole thing.

3. Visit a museum or art gallery. Talk with each other about the art you like and dislike. Use the "twenty questions" method to learn all you can about why your spouse likes or dislikes what you see.

4. Go to a driving range together. Cheer each other's good shots.

5. Go bowling together. Come up with prizes you can give each other for winning games: e.g., a massage, a week's worth of doing dishes, a promise to paint the fence, etc.

6. Go on a hayride with four other couples, singing camp songs from a tape recorder or guitar. Plan a cookout under the stars afterward.

7. Write love notes to one another and hide them in unusual places like the freezer, a shoe, in the car's glove box, in the bathtub, or under the bed covers.

8. Go snorkeling in a lake.

9. Collect leaves and pine cones together on an autumn day. Take them home and make fall ornaments for the house.

10. Attend a free outdoor concert.

11. Buy a pass from the Forest Service, go to a national forest, and cut your own Christmas tree if permitted.

12. Buy a modern paraphrase of the Song of Solomon and read it to one another.

13. Walk hand in hand along a nature trail.

14. Watch a sunset together.

15. Make "dough" ornaments together, bake them & then color them with the kids.

16. Rent each other's all-time favorite movies and play a double feature at home.

17. Go to your favorite restaurant for dessert. Bring a child's baby book or your wedding album and relive some memories together.

18. Throw a party commemorating your spouse's graduation date.

19. Get the children together and make a "Why I Love Mom" and "Why I Love Dad" book, complete with text and illustrations.

20. Take your wife out for an afternoon spent in her favorite store. Note the items under $20 she likes best. Return to the store the next day and buy one of those items as a gift.

(Love is a Decision, [Thomas Nelson, 1989] pages 141-143)

# Have You Become Your Parents?

Unhealthy relational patterns tend to be passed down from generation to generation, unless one makes a conscious effort to change course.

The ten questions in this inventory will help you judge where you've been so you can better judge where you are and where you should be in terms of relationship health. On a scale of 0 to 10, use the following statements to rate the way you were reared by your parents (0 = not at all; 10 = all the time).

My parents were

_____like dictators, demanding obedience.

_____rigid, forceful with strict rules, values, beliefs, and expectations (shamed us if we differed).

_____critical, judgmental with harsh punishment. ("I felt abused emotionally, sexually, physically, mentally, or spiritually.")

_____closed to talking about certain subjects: sex, religion, politics, and feelings.

_____poor listeners about my thoughts and feelings.

_____like a machine with many demands ("you should" and "you should not").

_____degrading with names such as "stupid," "lazy," "no good."

_____cold and indifferent toward me.

_____resistant to changes and learning new things. (It was not easy to disagree with them and stay "safe.")

_____distant (not close friends, and I was not invited to do things with them regularly).

Total your score. Add up the numbers of your ten responses. The higher your score (the closer it is to the max of 100), the higher the potential for your having been raised in an emotionally unhealthy home.

(*Making Love Last Forever* [Thomas Nelson, 1997], pages 138-139)

105

# Dear Gary....the 4-Day Q & A

You're not alone in the challenges and pressures within your relationship. Sometimes you look around and wonder if anyone else has the same problems you and your spouse do. In his many years counseling and having seminars with couples in crisis, Gary Smalley has often addressed some of the more common issues or stresses for a couple.

These include:

1. Feeling a loss of love
2. Only receiving conditional love
3. We just can't get along
4. Everything turns into an argument
5. Making sincere apologies

The following couples asked Gary for his insight and wisdom on these challenges. We hope you find similar encouragement and hope in Gary's responses.

## Feeling a loss of love

Q: I have been married for two and a half years and I feel that my wife no longer loves me. She is so emotionally detached. You talk about respecting a person's walls. How do you do that, yet work on opening her back up to work on our marriage?

A: In years past I've verbally violated my way into many of my most valued relationships. I was like a tank smashing down the protective and sometimes fragile walls around my wife's heart. Even if she wouldn't let me in, I'd say, "I'll come in anytime I want, and you'll like it."

Now I'm learning how to knock on Norma's gate first and see if she wants me to visit her concerning something serious, time-consuming, or critical.

People are too precious to jump over their walls without permission. It may cause serious hurt; often we never know how much until years later. Your wife has fences that protect her privacy or need for emotional space. Respecting these boundaries shows her that you honor her requests. Smashing down her walls won't work. It only makes the walls stronger.

Let her call the shots without always having to explain or defend herself to you. They are her walls, not yours. You are not solely responsible for creating them, so allow her the freedom and security to tear them down.

Practice softness. It's impossible to develop a satisfying deep emotionally based relationship without both persons feeling SAFE with each other. Her walls are a sign of her not feeling safe with you. Work on creating safety with her. The safer she feels, the sooner the walls will come down.

# Only receiving conditional love

**Q:** My husband and I have been married for six years and both are involved strongly in our church. During our marriage I have struggled with and gained weight. My husband has become very distant and has told me "You need to lose weight! I don't like it!" I do my best to eat healthy and stay away from junk food 95% of the time. I know I haven't exercised enough but started hitting the gym daily a couple of weeks ago. He sees that I am trying but is still distant. He constantly mentions the young pretty women he works with and is not acting toward me the way he used to. My self-esteem is gone. I pray, pray, pray. He promises me there is no one else. I am sad and confused!

**A:** Let me start by saying that you and your weight are not the issues here. Getting healthy and taking care of your body are both good things. But from what you have described, your health is not the concern. When we say that the issue is not the issue, we mean that there is an emotion hidden behind the issue. For instance,

- Is your husband worried for your health and quality of life?
- Is he embarrassed to be seen with you or uncomfortable making love to you?
- Is he disconnected because he is interested in other women?

Your weight is not the real issue. The reality is you could lose the weight and wear a size 2 or 4 dress and he may still be uninterested in you, especially if he is involved with other women. Your husband needs to deal with his own issues and his heart. All I can do is help you with your heart. Do not allow your husband's heart to keep you from growing in the Lord. As a child of God, you are loved. His love is not based on your bathroom scale.

You and I have the same choice to make—and our choice will largely determine whether we enjoy deep, satisfying relationships, or fragile, disappointing ones. I can't stress enough how crucial it is that each of us takes personal responsibility for how we think and respond within all of our relationships.

By nature, most of us want to blame those who upset us. We work hard to try to get them to change how they treat us. We attempt in many unhealthy ways to manipulate them. In the end, we wind up feeling hurt, abused, estranged, and lonely—and yet another relationship takes a tragic turn for the worse.

> Know today that you are unconditionally loved by God!

To take personal responsibility means that you refuse to focus on what the other person has done or said. You cannot change your husband's approach any more than he can change your weight.

# We just can't get along

**Q:** I married too young. We did not have enough time to get to know each other. I was more in love with the idea of the wedding and "being married" than I do living day in and day out with a guy who is my exact opposite. We are constantly annoying and frustrating each other. Can two people so different go the distance and make it a lifetime in marriage?

**A:** You've heard the saying "opposites attract," but in marriage it's usually "opposites attack." During pre-marital counseling, couples will often talk about all they have in common. This is because in the first stage of a relationship couples tend to overemphasize the things they have in common and underestimate their differences.

While dating, I assumed Norma would always love my fun-loving, easy-going, big-dreaming personality. I appreciated her uniqueness and skill with numbers and details. While we were dating, the contrast of our differences was fun and gave us plenty to talk about.

Once married, the similarities were downplayed and the differences were magnified. Now, over 40 years later our personalities have not changed. Norma and I are very different. Marriage is only one part of it. Working with your mate has a whole new set of challenges. My personality only sees big picture possibilities and Norma loves the nuts and bolts of how it all will work. Underestimated differences can create tension.

Marriage is much like a boat, and the differences between us are like icebergs floating up ahead. We can see the surface of the berg, but what we can't see may be ten times larger. Overlooking or underestimating differences can sink us if we're not careful. Do not neglect your differences. Have a reasonable estimate of each one's differences and how that plays out in your marriage. Raise the value of your mate by making a list of all of the positive qualities in him. Let the list grow over the years. It is too easy to focus on the negatives or differences and forget about the positives. Focus on the qualities that are honorable. And yes, you can go the distance!

# Everything turns into an argument

Q: Every conversation we have as a couple turns into a heated argument. Date nights get ruined constantly by deep conversations. We have lost the fun and laughter we had early in dating and marriage. We need help getting back on track.

A: If every outing you take ends up in heated conversation, declare a break from serious conversation. That communicates that you each need your down time. You need periods of time where you do not take yourselves so seriously. Learn to laugh with each other. Light-hearted evenings are great stress relievers. Two leading marriage experts have found that a marriage that thrives and last over 50 years has a 5 to 1 ratio of positive experiences to negative ones. So they advise that you make all of your date nights and trips together free of arguments. Sign a short contract between you that there will be no fights or angry arguments while you're having fun and kicking back together. That agreement will add to the ratio of the "5 to 1" positive experiences. Try changing your language toward each other.

| Some typical statements wives have told me they enjoy hearing: | Some typical statements husbands have told me they enjoy hearing: |
| --- | --- |
| "What a meal! M-m-m-m … that was delicious." | "Hey honey, why don't you call some buddies this weekend to hang out. You deserve it." |
| "I loved how you looked last night." | "I'll take care of the kids tonight; you go watch the game." |
| "Our kids are really blessed to have a mother like you. You take such good care of them." | "Thanks for letting me go shopping this weekend. I appreciated the little extra spending money." |
| "I don't know if I prefer the dress or what's in it better." | "The yard looks phenomenal. Who taught you how to stripe a yard?" |
| "Do I like your hairstyle? I'd like any hairstyle you have just because it's on you." | "I look forward to you being home tonight." |
| "Honey, you've worked so hard. Why don't you sit down and rest for a while before dinner? I can wait." | "The kids wanted me to call and tell you that you are the best daddy in the whole wide world." |

Simple, non-abrasive language goes a long way in restoring the love and kindness you once experienced.

109

# Making sincere apologies

**Q:** My wife says that I am one of the fastest apologizers she knows. She says the speed and repetition of my apologies voids the sincerity. She believes that when I say, "I'm sorry" it is just to get out of a fight. I can't win. Any suggestions?

Proverbs 16:24

**A:** Become a great wordsmith. Find new words and ways to say "I'm sorry."

When you use the right words, loving words, you change the atmosphere of your relationship. Proverbs says, "Gracious words are a honeycomb, sweet to the soul and healing to the bones" (Proverbs 16:24).

Put some thought into your apology. Be specific. Instead of a simple "I'm sorry," make it more of a complete sentence. "I'm sorry for snapping at you in the car earlier." "I'm sorry for being late again. I'm going to try harder to get home on time." "I'm sorry that I was an idiot earlier."

When you give the reason for your apology you communicate that you understand the frustration. The hidden marriage manual in every woman knows when the apology is given to claim the hurt or to simply smooth something over.

We all need to learn to settle accounts quickly and with clarity of thought.

As you have read in *4 Days to a Forever Marriage*, so much of the conflict or dysfunction in a relationship centers around how we respond to love and anger in a relationship. With the insights and skills learned through this book, you have empowered yourself and your spouse to make the right choices to nurture the loving, lifelong commitment you desire! May the Lord bless you in your journey!

111

#4days2forever
@GaryTSmalley

# Connect with twitter

*Follow* – @forevermarriage for tweets from
the book, encouragement from the authors & more

*Find* "Forever Marriage" Tweets throughout the
book. Share them online and inspire others to create a
"forever marriage" for themselves.

*Become* part of the Forever Marriage
community by adding this hashtag to your tweets
from and about the book –#4days2forever.

*Visit* http://search.twitter.com and enter
#4days2forever to meet others reading the book.

Facebook fans of the *4 Days to a Forever Marriage*
will have access to special features of the book
online, get the latest news on the Smalley's *4 Days
to a Forever Marriage* book specials and events. Like
our page now; go to:

Facebook.com/aforevermarriage